Giving Up the Ghost

A MEMOIR

Giving Up the Ghost

A MEMOIR

HILARY MANTEL

FOURTH ESTATE • *London* and *New York*

First published in Great Britain in 2003 by
Fourth Estate
A Division of HarperCollins*Publishers*
77–85 Fulham Palace Road
London W6 8JB
www.4thestate.com

3 5 7 9 10 8 6 4 2

The lines from *Carolina Ghost Woods*, by Judy Jordan, are published by
kind permission of the author and the Louisiana State University Press.

The right of Hilary Mantel to be identified as the author of this work
has been asserted by her in accordance with the Copyright,
Designs and Patents Act 1988.

A catalogue record for this book is available from the British Library

ISBN 0-00-714841-0

Typeset in Bell by Palimpsest Book Production Limited,
Polmont, Stirlingshire
Printed and bound in Great Britain by
Clays Ltd, St Ives plc

For my family

Small holes, secret graves,
children scattered around the iron fence.
Not even a scratched stone.

The wind rises, clouds cover the moon,
a dog's bark and those owls,
Alone and no end.

My children who won't hear.
The night full of cries they will never make.

'Sharecropper's Grave'
Judy Jordan

Contents

PART ONE

A Second Home

It is a Saturday, late July, 2000; we are in Reepham, Norfolk, at Owl Cottage. There's something we have to do today, but we are trying to postpone it. We need to go across the road to see Mr Ewing; we need to ask for a valuation, and see what they think of our chances of selling. Ewing's are the local firm, and it was they who sold us the house, seven years ago. As the morning wears on we move around each other silently, avoiding conversation. The decision's made. There's no more to discuss.

About eleven o'clock, I see a flickering on the staircase. The air is still; then it moves. I raise my head. The air is still again. I know it is my stepfather's ghost coming down. Or, to put it in a way acceptable to most people, I 'know' it is my stepfather's ghost.

I am not perturbed. I am used to 'seeing' things that aren't there. Or – to put it in a way more acceptable to me – I am used to seeing things that 'aren't there'. It was in this house that I last saw my stepfather Jack, in the early months of 1995: alive, in his garments of human flesh. Many times since then I have acknowledged him on the stairs.

It may be, of course, that the flicker against the banister was nothing more than the warning of a migraine attack. It's at the left-hand side of my body that visions manifest; it's my left eye that is peeled. I don't know whether, at such vulnerable times, I see more than is there; or if things are there, that normally I don't see.

Over the years the premonitionary symptoms of migraine headaches have become more than the dangerous puzzle that they were earlier in my life, and more than a warning to take the drugs that might ward off a full-blown attack. They have become a psychic adornment or flourish, an art form, a secret talent I have never managed to make money from. Sometimes they take the form of the visual disturbances that are common to many sufferers. Small objects will vanish from my field of vision, and there will be floating lacunae in the world, each shaped rather like a doughnut with a dazzle of light where the hole should be. Sometimes there are flashes of gold against the wall: darting chevrons, like the wings of small quick angels. Scant sleep and lack of food increase the chances of these sightings; starving saints in Lent, hypoglycemic and jittery, saw visions to meet their expectations.

Sometimes the aura takes more trying forms. I will go deaf. The words I try to write end up as other words. I will suffer strange dreams, from which I wake with hallucinations of taste. Once, thirty years ago, I dreamt that I was eating bees, and ever since I have lived with their milk-chocolate sweetness and their texture, which is like lightly cooked calves' liver. It may be that a tune will lodge in my head like a tic and bring the words tripping in with it, so I am forced to live my life by its accompaniment. It's a familiar complaint, to have a tune you can't get out of your head. But for most people the tunes aren't the prelude to a day of hearty vomiting. Besides, people say they pick them up from the radio, but mine are songs people don't really sing these days: Bill Bailey, won't you please come home? Some talk of Alexander, and some of Hercules. My aged father did me deny, And the name he gave me was the croppy boy.

Today, the day I see the ghost, the problem's just that my words don't come out right. So I have to be careful, at Mr Ewing's, but he understands me without any trouble, and yes, he remembers selling us the cottage, seven years ago, is it really so long? They were years in which perhaps half a million words were drafted and redrafted, seven and a half thousand meals were consumed, ten thousand painkillers (at a conservative estimate) were downed by me, and God knows how many by the people I'd given a pain; years in which I got fatter and fatter (wider still and wider, shall my bounds be set): and during seven years of nights, dreams were dreamt, then erased or re-formatted: they were years during which, on the eve of the publication of my seventh novel, my stepfather died. All my memories of him are bound up with houses, dreams of houses, real or dream houses with empty rooms waiting for occupation: with other people's stories, and other people's claims: with fright and my adult denial that I was frightened. But affection takes strange forms, after all. I can hardly bear to sell the cottage and leave him behind on the stairs.

Late in the afternoon, a migrainous sleep steals up on me. It plants on my forehead a clammy ogre's kiss. 'Don't worry,' I say, as the ogre sucks me into sleep. 'If the phone wakes, it will ring us.' I knew the migraine was coming yesterday, when I stood in a Norfolk fishmonger choosing a treat for the cats. 'No,' I said, 'cod's too expensive just now to feed to fish. Even fish like ours.'

I hardly know how to write about myself. Any style you pick seems to unpick itself before a paragraph is done. I will just go for it, I think to myself, I'll hold out my hands and say, *c'est moi*, get used to it. I'll trust the reader. This is what I recommend to people who ask me how to get published. Trust your reader, stop spoon-feeding your reader, stop patronising your reader, give your reader credit for being as smart as you at least, and stop being so bloody beguiling: you in the back row, will you turn off that charm! Plain words on plain paper. Remember what Orwell says, that good prose is like a window-pane. Concentrate on sharpening your memory and peeling your sensibility. Cut every page you write by at least one-third. Stop constructing those piffling little similes of yours. Work out what it is you want to say. Then say it in the most direct and vigorous way you can. Eat meat. Drink blood. Give up your social life and don't think you can have friends. Rise in the quiet hours of the night and prick your fingertips, and use the blood for ink; that will cure you of persiflage!

But do I take my own advice? Not a bit. Persiflage is my *nom de guerre*. (Don't use foreign expressions; it's élitist.) I stray away from the beaten path of plain words into the meadows of extravagant simile: angels, ogres, doughnut-shaped holes. And as for transparency – window-panes undressed are a sign of poverty, aren't they? How about some nice net curtains, so I can look out but you can't see in? How about shutters, or a chaste Roman blind? Besides, window-pane prose is no guarantee of truthfulness. Some deceptive sights are seen through glass, and the best liars tell lies in plain words.

So now I come to write a memoir I argue with myself over every word. Is my writing clear: or is it deceptively clear? I tell myself, just say how you came to sell a house with a ghost in it. But this story can be told only once, and I need to get it right. Why does the act of writing generate so much anxiety?

Margaret Atwood says, 'The written word is so much like evidence – like something that can be used against you.' I used to think that autobiography was a form of weakness, and perhaps I still do. But I also think that, if you're weak, it's childish to pretend to be strong.

Sell Owl: the decision came with us, crawling through the Friday-evening traffic on the M25, and navigating the darkness of Breckland settlements with their twisted pines and shuttered houses. We had done this journey so many times, looping past the centre of Norwich on the fringes of industrial estates, slowing at the crossroads among West Earlham council houses: lamps burning behind drawn curtains, no one in the streets. As you cross the city boundary the street lights run out, the road narrows. You creep forward into that darkness which is lit only by the glittering eyes of foxes and farm cats, which is punctuated by the flurry of wing-beats and scurrying of busy feet in the verges. Something unseen is eating. Something is being consumed.

As you enter the small town of Reepham you turn by the church wall, bashed and battered by many long vehicles, into the market place empty of cars. The King's Arms is still burning a light, the big doors of the Old Brewery are closed and its residents padding upwards to their beds. Turning uphill from the square, you park on the muddy rutted ground at the back of the cottage, unloading in the dark and mostly in the rain; your boots know the puddles and slippery patches, the single dark step and the paving's edge. Sometimes it is midnight and winter, the cold sucking the virtue from a torch beam, diffusing the light into an aimless dazzle. But just as feet know the path, fingers know the keys. Fifty yards from the market place there is no light pollution, no urban backwash to pale the sky; no flight path, no footfall. There is starlight, frost on the path, and owls crying from three parishes.

You sleep well in this house, though if you are here on a weekday morning the trucks and tractors wake you at dawn. Their exudates plaster the roadside windows with a greasy, smearing dirt. The country is not clean or quiet. Through the day hydraulic brakes wheeze as truck drivers come to halt at the bottom of the hill, at Townsend Corner. But when they say town's end, they mean it. Beyond the police station, beyond the last bungalow – that is to say, in less than a quarter of a mile – the town becomes open fields. The next settlement is Kerdiston. Its church fell down several hundred years ago. It has no street names and indeed, no streets. Even the people who live there aren't sure where it is. Its single distinguished resident, Sir William de Kerdeston, moved to Reepham after he died, and lies in effigy on his tomb, resting – if that is the word – in full armour and on a bed of pebbles: his shoulder muscles twitching, perhaps, his legs flexing, every year as we reach the Feast of All Souls and the dead prepare to walk.

When we bought the cottage it had no name or history. It was a conversion of buildings that might once have been a house, or not; most likely it was some kind of agricultural storeroom. At some point early in the 1990s, a Norwich builder knocked four flats and two cottages out of its undistinguished structure of old red-brown brick.

In the winter of 1992–93 we were scouring the county for a weekend place. We went to the coast and deep into the heartland, always keeping in mind the long journey from Berkshire and our need to settle, for weekends, close to my parents, who had retired to Holt. Studded into our Barbours, driving our scarlet BMW, we were a sight to gladden the eyes of any country estate agent. We would see their faces light up, only to assume their habitual grey glaze when we introduced them to our stringent budget and our high requirements. We wanted nothing tumbledown, nothing picturesque, nothing with a small but containable dry rot problem. And nothing too remote, as I might want to stay there alone, and I am myself too remote and nervous and irritable to drive a car. We wanted a shop and a pub, but most Norfolk villages are straggling depopulated hamlets, with a telephone box, if you're lucky, to mark their centre. All the same, we thought there was a home for us somewhere in the county. I'd just won a book prize, so we had unexpected cash to pitch in. Norfolk wasn't fashionable then. People thought it was too far from London, and it didn't have what urbanites require, the infrastructure of gourmet dining and darling little delis; it had pubs that served microwaved baked potatoes with huge glum portions of gravy and meat, and small branches of Woolworths in small towns, and Spar groceries in larger villages, and water birds, and long reaches of shingle and sea, and a vast expanse of painter's sky.

By this stage we knew Norfolk fairly well. I had first come to the county in 1980, to stay with friends who were themselves newly settled in a Broadlands village. My own home was in Africa, but my marriage was breaking up. A wan child with a suitcase – an old child, at twenty-eight – I went about to visit people, to stay for a while and drift away again, ending up always back at my parental home, which was then still in the north. I seemed to be perpetually on trains, dragging my luggage up flights of steps at Crewe, or trying to find a sheltered place on the windswept platforms of Nuneaton. As I travelled, I grew thinner and thinner, more frayed and shabby, more lonely. I was homesick for the house I had left, for my animals, for the manuscript of the vast novel I had written and left behind. I was homesick for my husband, but my feelings about my past were too impenetrable and misty for me to grasp, and to keep them that way I often began and ended each day with a sprinkling of barbiturates gulped from my palm, washed down with the water from some other household's cup. When you take barbiturates at night your dreams are blank and black, and your awakening is sick and distant, the day in front of you like a shoreline glimpsed from a pitching ship. But this is because you need another dose. After an hour, you feel just fine.

My Norfolk host was a woman I had known in Africa. Her husband was working abroad again, and she didn't like to be alone in the country dark. If our strained expatriate lives had not brought us into contact, we would never have been friends; after a while I realised we weren't friends anyway, so I got on a train in Norwich and never came back. But our long drives about the county, lost in winter lanes, our limp salads in village cafés, our scramblings in overgrown churchyards and our attention to the stories of old people had made me think deeply about this territory, and want to write a novel set there. After some years, this was what I did.

We had been separated for no more than two years when my ex-husband came to England, changed. I believe people do change; there's no mileage, really, in believing the opposite. I also had changed. I was living alone. I was sick with a chronic illness, swollen by steroid medication, and a cynic in matters of romance. Of Freud's two constants, love and work, I now embraced just one; I was employed six days a week at two ill-paid jobs, days in a bookshop and nights behind a bar, and I got up at dawn to write my journals and stabilise my body for a venture into the world. I kept notes for future books; at that time, 1982, I had published only one short story. I had given up barbiturates. I don't remember exactly when I stopped, or what I did with the endless supply of tiny pills from the big plastic tub I'd brought from Africa. Did I tail them off? Stop them cold? I don't know. In view of the claims I will later make for my memory, this causes me concern. Perhaps they brought their own oblivion with them, each rattling little scoop of pinhead-sized killers. Since then I have always been addicted to something or other, usually something there's no support group for. Semicolons, for instance, I can never give up for more than two hundred words at a time.

Whether I was fit, that summer, to take a rational decision – well, who ever knows about that? It seemed that what I had left, with my ex-husband, was more than most people started with. So we got married again, economically, at the registrar's office in Maidenhead, with two witnesses. It was September, and I felt very ill that morning, queasy and swollen, as if I were pregnant; there was a pain behind my diaphragm, and from time to time something seemed to flip over and claw at me, as if I were a woman in a folk tale, pregnant with a demon. Nothing, except for having to get married, would have got me out of bed, into my dress, into my high heels and into the street. The registrar was kindly and wished us better luck this time around. There was no ring; as the size of my fingers was changing week to week, I didn't see the point, and it is possible, also, that I didn't want to resume the signs and symbols of marriage too quickly. We had lunch in a restaurant in Windsor, in a courtyard overlooking the river. We had champagne. A witness took a photograph, in which I look hollow-eyed, like a turnip lantern. This is how – I have to shake myself to say it – I have been married twice: twice to the same man. I always thought it was a film people pursuit, or what peroxided pools winners used to do, dippy people destabilised by good fortune. I thought it was what people did when they had stormy temperaments; it was not an enterprise for the prudent or steadfast. Though perhaps, if you're prudent and steadfast past a certain point, it's the only reasonable thing to do. You would go on getting married and married to that person, marrying and marrying them, for as many times as it needed to make it stick.

*　　*　　*

In mid-January 1993 we made our headquarters at the
Blakeney Hotel, a flint ship sailing the salt marshes.
We were equipped with sheaves of property details,
most of them lying or misleading. For two days we
drove the lanes, crossing houses off as soon as we saw
their location or exterior. I was recovering from a bad
Christmas – bronchitis and a lung inflammation – and
I had no voice. But voice was not necessary, only an
ability to peer at the map in fading light and at the
same time monitor faded fingerposts, leaning under
the weight of Norfolk place names. At five on a Sunday
afternoon, in near-dark, we were up to our calves
in mud somewhere east of East Dereham, a stone's
throw from an ancient crumbling church and a row
of tumbledown corrugated-iron farm buildings, trying
to find a track to a forlorn little cottage at the end of
a forlorn little row. We gave it up, sat disconsolate
inside the scarlet monster, and turned our minds to
the M25.

When we returned, still in bitter weather, I had got
my voice back and we had narrowed our search. Often,
when I was staying with my friend from Africa, we had
come to Reepham to shop, and I had looked up at the
long Georgian windows of the Old Brewery. It was
a pub and small hotel, an elegant red-brick building
with a sundial and that Latin inscription which means
'I only count the happy hours'. By the time I returned
there, ten years on, Reepham had a post office, two

butchers, a pharmacy, as well as a telephone kiosk: a hairdresser, one or two discreet antique dealers, a busy baker's shop which sold vitamins and farm eggs and organic chocolate, and a greengrocer-florist called Meloncaulie Rose. A well-arranged town square was surrounded by calm, wide-windowed houses, and a jumble of cottages tumbling down Station Road. There was no longer a station, though in Victorian times there had been two, and twelve beer houses, and a cattle market. There had been three churches, but one of them burnt down in 1543, and was never rebuilt; the history of the town is of a slow decline into impiety, and abstemiousness. On a January day, after I became a resident, a huddled old lady beckoned me from her doorway, and looked across the deserted market place to the church gates. 'What do you make of it?' she said. 'More life in the churchyard than in the street today.'

The people of Reepham and the surrounding villages gather in the post office on a Saturday morning. They discuss rainfall – 'not enough to wet a stamp,' I once heard a man say. They talk about whether they have put their heating on, or switched it off, and about nonagenarian drivers who crawl the lanes in their Morris Travellers. They are not inhospitable. They don't make a stranger of you till you've lived there for twenty years. They don't in fact make much of you at all. People once employed on the land are now quite likely to work at a computer terminal. They don't know you, but they don't mind that. They're live and let live. They used to greet each other with 'Are you all right?' a question with a unique Norfolk inflection, but they don't do that so much as they did. They go into their houses early on Christmas Eve, and lock the doors. They leave their windfall apples and overproduce of vegetables outside their doors in baskets, for anyone to take, and sell bunches of daffodils for pennies in the spring.

When we went to see the house, the builder's debris was still in it. We stood in its unfinished rooms and imagined it. We imagined it would be ours. It was cheap, and a minute from the market place. At midnight, we left our room at the Old Brewery and walked to the gate: or to where the gate would be. We wanted to see it again, in privacy and silence. As we stood, hunched into our coats on a night of obdurate cold, the tawny owl called out from the tree.

Later we had a plaque made to say 'Owl Cottage', with a picture. But the man did a barn owl, canary yellow and thin, with creepy feet like the feet of a rodent.

It's a strange phenomenon, the 'second home'. Like the second marriage, it's not something that I ever associated with myself. I thought it was for rich people who drove up prices in the Cotswolds. I never felt guilty about Owl Cottage; there was hardly a queue for it, with its tiny backyard and weekday traffic noise. We hoped that buying it would be the first stage of a permanent move to Norfolk. Getting into our car, the BMW and its less flashy successors, I would imagine this was the final journey, and that we were travelling in convoy with the removal van: that we were leaving the South-east behind for ever. When I played this game, I would smile and my shoulders would relax. But then we would grind to a halt, at the sight of some carnage or disaster on the M25, and I would have to acknowledge that it was just another short, fraught weekend trip, and that the change in our lives would have to be earned.

For a time, we would visit every two or three weeks, our two cats travelling with us. Released, squalling, from their cage, they would race through the rooms, bellowing, feet thundering on the wooden stairs, driving out the devils only cats can see. Exhausted, they would take to their basket, while we climbed the stairs to a room papered the pale yellow of weak sunshine: better people already, calmer, kinder. On Saturday morning we would make a leisurely circuit of the market place, shop to shop, talking to people, posting our parcels, filling my many prescriptions, buying meat for our freezer. In the afternoon we would drive up to Holt to see my parents, with a bag of scones or a cake, some flowers, a book or two; then on Sunday my parents would drive to Reepham, and we would have lunch at the King's Arms or eat something cold at home: Cromer crabs, strawberries, Stilton. Then it was time to pack the car and go. Routinely, as we left, there was a small ache behind my ribs. I only count the happy hours.

My mother was a tiny, chic woman with a shaggy bob of platinum-coloured hair. She usually wore jeans and a mad-coloured sweatshirt, but everything she wore looked designed and meant; all the time I'd known her, since first I'd been able to see her clearly, she'd had that knack. My stepfather was younger than she was, by a few years, but he had undergone a coronary bypass, and his brown, muscular body seemed wasted. Frail, was not a word I would have associated with him, but I noticed how his favourite shirt, soft and faded, clung to his ribs, and his legs seemed to consist of his trousers with articulated sticks inside. Once a draughtsman, he had taken up watercolours, trying to fix on to paper the troubling, shifting colours of the coast; earlier in life, he would not have been able to tolerate the ambiguities and tricks of the light. Passion had wasted him, and anger; no one had given him a helping hand, he had no money when money mattered, and he was chronically exasperated by the evasions and crookedness of the world. He was honest by temperament; the honest, in this world, give each other a hard time. He was an engineer. He wrote a small, exact, engineer's hand, and his mind was subdued to a discipline, but inside his chest his heart would knock about, like a wasp in an inverted glass.

I had been six or seven when Jack had first entered my life. In all those years, we had never had a proper conversation. I felt that I had nothing to say that would interest him; I don't know what he felt. Neither of us could make small talk. For my part, it made me tense, as if there were hidden meanings in it, and for his part . . . for his part I don't know. My mother thought we didn't get on because we were too much alike, but I preferred the obvious explanation, that we didn't get on because we were completely different.

Now, this situation began to change. Since his heart surgery, Jack had shown a more open and flexible personality than ever in his life. He had become more patient, more equable, less taciturn: and so I, in his presence, had become less guarded, more grown-up, more talkative. I found that I could entertain him with stories of the writers' committees I sat on in London; he had been a man who sat on committees, before his enforced retirement, and we agreed that whatever they were for ostensibly, all committees behaved alike, and could probably be trusted to transact each other's business. On that last afternoon, a bright fresh day towards the end of March, I hung back as we crossed the market place, so that my husband and my mother would walk ahead, and I could have a moment to tell him some small thing that only he would like. I thought, I have never done that before: never hung back, never waited for him.

He seemed tired, when we got home after the meal. One of the cats, the striped one, used to lure him to play with her on the stairs. Until recently, he had loathed cats, denounced them like a Witchfinder General; he claimed to shrink at their touch. But this tiny animal, with her own strange phobias, fright shivering behind her marzipan eyes, would invite him with an upraised paw to put out his hand for her to touch; and he would oblige her, held there by her mewing for ten minutes at a time, touching and retreating, pushed away and fetched back.

That last Sunday, when she took up her stance and invited him to begin, he stayed on the sofa, smiling at her and nodding. I thought, perhaps he is sickening for something: flu? But it was death he was sickening for, and it came suddenly, death the plunderer, uncouth and foul-mouthed, kicking his way into their house on a night in April two or three hours before dawn. The doctor came and the ambulance crew, but death had arrived before them, his feet planted on the hearthrug, his filthy fingerprints on the pillowcase. They did their best, but they could have done their worst, for all it availed. When everything was signed and certified, my mother said, and the men had gone away, she washed his face. She sat by his body and because there was no one to talk to she sang in a low voice: 'What's this dull town to me?/ Robin's not near/ He whom I wished to see/Wished for to hear . . .'

She sang this song to me when I was small: the tune is supersaturated with yearning, with longing for a lost love. About six o'clock she moved to the phone, but all her three children were sleeping soundly, and so she received only polite requests to leave the message that no one can ever leave. On and on we slept. 'Where's all the joy and mirth/ Made life a heaven on earth?/ O they're all fled with thee/ Robin Adare.' About seven o'clock, at last, one of my brothers picked up the phone.

You come to this place, mid-life. You don't know how you got here, but suddenly you're staring fifty in the face. When you turn and look back down the years, you glimpse the ghosts of other lives you might have led. All your houses are haunted by the person you might have been. The wraiths and phantoms creep under your carpets and between the warp and weft of your curtains, they lurk in wardrobes and lie flat under drawer liners. You think of the children you might have had but didn't. When the midwife says 'It's a boy,' where does the girl go? When you think you're pregnant, and you're not, what happens to the child that has already formed in your mind? You keep it filed in a drawer of your consciousness, like a short story that wouldn't work after the opening lines.

In the February of 2002, my godmother Maggie fell ill, and hospital visits took me back to my native village. After a short illness she died, at the age of almost ninety-five, and I returned again for her funeral. I had been back many times over the years, but on this occasion there was a particular route I had to take: down the winding road between the hedgerows and the stone wall, and up a wide unmade track which, when I was small, people called 'the carriage drive'. It leads uphill to the old school, now disused, then to the convent, where there are no nuns these days, then to the church. When I was a child this was my daily walk, once in the morning to school and once again to school after dinner – that meal which the south of England calls lunch. Retracing it as an adult, in my funeral black, I felt a sense of oppression, powerful and familiar. Just before the public road joins the carriage drive came a point where I was overwhelmed by fear and dismay. My eyes moved sideways, in dread, towards dank vegetation, tangled bracken: I wanted to say, stop here, let's go no further. I remembered how when I was a child, I used to think I might bolt, make a run for it, scurry back to the (comparative) safety of home. The point where fear overcame me was the point of no turning back.

Each month, from the age of seven to my leaving

at eleven, we walked in crocodile up the hill from the school to the church to go to confession and be forgiven for our sins. I would come out of church feeling, as you would expect, clean and light. This period of grace never lasted beyond the five minutes it took to get inside the school building. From about the age of four I had begun to believe I had done something wrong. Confession didn't touch some essential sin. There was something inside me that was beyond remedy and beyond redemption. The school's work was constant stricture, the systematic crushing of any spontaneity. It enforced rules that had never been articulated, and which changed as soon as you thought you had grasped them. I was conscious, from the first day in the first class, of the need to resist what I found there. When I met my fellow children and heard their yodelling cry – 'Good mo-or-orning, Missis Simpson,' I thought I had come among lunatics; and the teachers, malign and stupid, seemed to me like the lunatics' keepers. I knew you must not give in to them. You must not answer questions which evidently had no answer, or which were asked by the keepers simply to amuse themselves and pass the time. You must not accept that things were beyond your understanding because they told you they were; you must go on trying to understand them. A state of inner struggle began. It took a huge expenditure of energy to keep your own thoughts intact. But if you did not make this effort you would be wiped out.

Before I went to school there was a time when I was happy, and I want to write down what I remember about that time. The story of my own childhood is a complicated sentence that I am always trying to finish, to finish and put behind me. It resists finishing, and partly this is because words are not enough; my early world was synaesthesic, and I am haunted by the ghosts of my own sense impressions, which re-emerge when I try to write, and shiver between the lines.

We are taught to be chary of early memories. Sometimes psychologists fake photographs in which a picture of their subject, in his or her childhood, appears in an unfamiliar setting, in places or with people whom in real life they have never seen. The subjects are amazed at first but then – in proportion to their anxiety to please – they oblige by producing a 'memory' to cover the experience that they have never actually had. I don't know what this shows, except that some psychologists have persuasive personalities, that some subjects are imaginative, and that we are all told to trust the evidence of our senses, and we do it: we trust the objective fact of the photograph, not our subjective bewilderment. It's a trick, it isn't science; it's about our present, not about our past. Though my early memories are patchy, I think they are not, or not entirely, a confabulation, and I believe this because of their overwhelming sensory power; they come complete, not like the groping, generalised formulations of the subjects fooled by the photograph. As I say 'I tasted', I taste, and as I say 'I heard', I hear: I am not talking about a Proustian moment, but a Proustian cine-film. Anyone can run these ancient newsreels, with a bit of preparation, a bit of practice; maybe it comes easier to writers than to many people, but I wouldn't be sure about that. I wouldn't agree either that it doesn't matter what you remember, but only what you think you remember. I have an investment in accuracy; I would never say, 'It doesn't matter, it's history now.' I know, on the other hand, that a small child has a strange sense of time, where a year seems a decade, and everyone over the age of ten seems grown-up and of an equal age; so although I feel sure of what happened, I am less sure of the sequence and the dateline. I know, too, that once a family has acquired a habit of secrecy, memories begin to distort, because its members confabulate to cover the gaps in the facts; you have to make some sort of sense of what's going on around you, so you cobble together a narrative as best you can. You add to it, and reason about it, and the distortions breed distortions.

Still, I think people can remember: a face, a perfume: one true thing or two. Doctors used to say babies didn't feel pain; we know they were wrong. We are born with our sensibilities; perhaps we are conceived that way. Part of our difficulty in trusting ourselves is that in talking of memory we are inclined to use geological metaphors. We talk about buried parts of our past and assume the most distant in time are the hardest to reach: that one has to prospect for them with the help of a hypnotist, or psychotherapist. I don't think memory is like that: rather that it is like St Augustine's 'spreading limitless room'. Or a great plain, a steppe, where all the memories are laid side by side, at the same depth, like seeds under the soil.

There is a colour of paint that doesn't seem to exist any more, that was a characteristic pigment of my childhood. It is a faded, rain-drenched crimson, like stale and drying blood. You saw it on panelled front doors, and on the frames of sash windows, on mill gates and on those high doorways that led to the ginnels between shops and gave access to their yards. You can still see it, on the more soot-stained and dilapidated old buildings, where the sandblaster hasn't yet been in to turn the black stone to honey: you can detect a trace of it, a scrape. The restorers of great houses use paint scrapes to identify the original colour scheme of old salons, drawing rooms and staircase halls. I use this paint scrape – oxblood, let's call it – to refurbish the rooms of my childhood: which were otherwise dark green, and cream, and more lately a cloudy yellow, which hung about at shoulder height, like the aftermath of a fire.

PART TWO

Now Geoffrey Don't Torment Her

Two of my relatives have died by fire. One was my father's mother, whose name was Alice.

Alice was a widow. She was preparing to marry again, but a short while before the ceremony she saw her dead husband in the street. She took this as a sign to call it off. A house fire killed her before I was born, even before my father married my mother. I've never seen her picture. She's gone.

The other victim of fire was from my mother's family. She was a little girl called Olive, who was burned to death when her nightdress caught alight. I know her because a photograph of her is set into a brooch. It is oval, which is the shape of melancholy, nostalgia and lost romance. It shows a childlike smudge, unformed, without expression. On the other side of the brooch is George Foster, my maternal grandfather. He is a young soldier, grave, handsome, intent. If you wear the brooch, he is the natural choice to turn outwards. No one, I guess, has ever put Olive on display. She gazes backwards for ever, blurred eyes on someone's breastbone; looking inside the body, like a child who has never left the womb.

This is the first thing I remember. I am sitting up in my pram. We are outside, in the park called Bankswood. My mother walks backwards. I hold out my arms because I don't want her to go. She says she's only going to take my picture. I don't understand why she goes backwards, back and aslant, tacking to one side. The trees overhead make a noise of urgent conversation, too quick to catch; the leaves part, the sky moves, the suns peers down at me. Away and away she goes, till she comes to a halt. She raises her arm and partly hides her face. The sky and trees rush over my head. I feel dizzied. The entire world is sound, movement. She moves towards me, speaking. The memory ends.

This memory exists now in black and white, because when I was older I saw Bankswood pictures: this photograph or similar ones, perhaps taken that day, perhaps weeks earlier, or weeks later. In the nineteen-fifties photographs often didn't come out at all, or were so fuzzy that they were thrown away. What remains as a memory, though the colour has bled away, is the fast scudding of clouds and the rush of sound over my head, the wind in the trees: as if the waters of life have begun to flow.

Many years later, when there was a suspicion about

my heart, I was sent to hospital for a test called an echocardiogram. A woman rolled me with a big roller. I heard the same sound, the vast, pulsing, universal roar: my own blood in my own veins. But for a time I didn't know whether that sound came from inside me, or from the depth of the machines by my bed.

I am learning, always learning. To take someone's picture, you move away from them. When you have finished, you move back.

The results of the test, I should say, were satisfactory. My heart was no bigger than one would expect.

I learn to walk in the house, but don't remember that. Outside the house, you turn left: I don't know it's left. Moving towards the next-door house: from my grandmother (56 Bankbottom, Hadfield, Near Manchester) to her elder sister, at no. 58. Embedded in the stonework on the left of my grandmother's door is a rusty iron ring. I always slip my finger into it, though I should not. Grandad says it is where they tied the monkey up, but I don't think they really ever had one; all the same, he lurks in my mind, a small grey monkey with piteous eyes and a long active tail.

I have taken my finger from the ring, and tasted it for metal. I am looking down at the paving stones beneath the window. I have to pass the length of that window before I arrive at no. 58. I keep my eyes on the narrow stones which, placed edge to edge, form a kerb. One, two, and the third is a raised, blueish stone, the colour of a bruise, and on this stone, perhaps because it is the colour of a bruise, I will fall and howl. Because I know I always, always cannot get past; and because howl is my stage of life, it is indulged in me. This goes on, till one day the consciousness of self-fulfilling prophecy enters my head. I decide I will not fall; I will not fall, and see what happens. I negotiate the bruise stone. It is the first time. Only once is needed. Now I can walk outside the house. I jump into the arms of my grandfather, George Foster, and I know I have nothing to fear.

At no. 58 the top of my head comes to the outermost curve of my great-aunt, Annie Connor. Her shape is like the full moon, her smile is beaming; the outer rim of her is covered by her pinny, woven with tiny flowers. It is soft from washing; her hands are hard and chapped; it is barely ten o'clock, and she is getting the cabbage on. 'Hello, Our Ilary,' she says; my family have named me aspirationally, but aspiration doesn't stretch to the 'H'. Rather embarrassed for her, that she hasn't spotted who I am, I slip her my name of the day. I claim I'm an Indian brave. I claim I'm Sir Launcelot. I claim I'm the parish priest and she doesn't quibble. I give her a blessing; she says, thank you Father.

My head comes above the keyboard of the black piano. When you press a key the sound is bronchial, damaged; the piano at no. 56 has a more mellow note. I know how to find middle 'C' because on the piano at no. 56 this key has a brown stain on the ivory, and a frill chipped out of it, as if some tiny animal has nibbled it. I am fond of the pianos, their two different voices and smells: the deep, disdainful, private aroma of their wood. Nobody has told me yet that I am disastrously unmusical and had better leave the pianos alone. If someone will play I will stand at the side with my fingers on the wood and feel the resonance, the piano breathing and purring like a cat. I do not know a cat. Tibby is Mrs Clayton's cat. He lives at no. 60, and flees along the wall. I do not know him. He is a Protestant cat. George Clayton is the first in the yard to rise in the morning, winter and summer long before dawn, treading from his house to the lavatory. I see him in the afternoon, coming home in broad day: a bulky figure in blue overalls, with a bulky blinkered head. One day he dies. Mrs Clayton, people say, is 'taken to Macclesfield': that is to say, she is mad. When she returns, the cat Tibby still flees along the wall. Instead of George, Mrs Clayton gets a blunt-headed dog called Shula. The dog's kennel name, she tells me, is Shula Ballerina. It snaps and snarls and hurtles about the backyard. This does not prevent her going mad again.

In no. 58, Annie Connor starts a game. You go into a corner of the room. She into another. You both shout, very loud:

The wind blows east,
The wind blows west,
The wind blows o'er yon cuckoo's nest.
Where is he
That has to go
Over yonder fields?
Hi Ho!

Then you just run about the room, screaming. So does she.

Two things not to believe: the monkey. People who say, 'I have eyes in the back of my head.'

I sit on the stairs, which are steep, box-like, dark. I think I am going to die. I have breathed in a housefly, I think I have. The fly was in the room and my mouth open because I was putting into it a sweet. Then the fly was nowhere to be seen. It manifests now as a tickling and scraping on the inside of my throat, the side of my throat that's nearest to the kitchen wall. I sit with my head down and my arms on my knees. Flies are universally condemned and said to be laden with filth, crawling with germs, therefore what more sure way to die than swallow or inhale one? There is another possibility, which I turn and examine in my brain: perhaps the tickling in my throat is the sweet itself, which is a green sweet from a box of assorted candy called Weekend. Probably I shouldn't have eaten this one, but a jelly kind or fudge, more suitable to a child, and if I had hesitated and said I want that marzipan someone would have said 'That's bad for you,' but now I'm on the stairs not knowing whether it's green sweet or fly. The fear of death stirs slowly within my chest cavity, like a stewpot lazily bubbling. I feel sorrow; I am going to miss seeing my grandparents and everyone else I know. I wonder whether I should mention the fact that I am dying, either from a fly or a green sweet. I decide to keep it to myself, as there won't be anything anyone can do. It will be kinder for them if they don't know; but I feel lonely, here on the stairs with my future shortening. I curse the moment I opened my mouth, and let the fly in. There is a rasping, tickling sensation deep in my throat, which I think is the fly rubbing its hands together. I begin to wonder how long it will take to die . . .

After a while I am walking about in the room again. My resolve to die completely alone has faltered. I suppose it will take an hour or so, or I might live till evening. My head is still hanging. What's the matter? I am asked. I don't feel I can say. My original intention was not to raise the alarm; also, I feel there is shame in such a death. I would rather just fall over, and that would be an end of it. I feel queasy now. Something is tugging at my attention. Perhaps it is a sense of absurdity. The dry rasping in my throat persists, but now I don't know if it is the original obstruction lodged there, or the memory of it, the imprint, which is not going to fade from my breathing flesh. For many years the word 'marzipan' affects me with its deathly hiss, the buzz in its syllables, a sepulchral fizz.

My grandad goes on to the Red Lamp to take a gill. He puts on his checked sports coat and I shout, 'Grandad is wearing his beer jacket.' He puts on his suede shoes and I shout, 'Grandad has put on his beer shoes.' He takes up the pitcher from the kitchen shelf and I shout, 'Grandad is taking his beer jug.' However mild his habits, however temperate, I can't be stopped from chronicling his deeds.

The likes of a woman wouldn't go in the Red Lamp.

My grandfather knows about English things such as Robin Hood. I sit on his knee as he hums 'All things bright and beautiful'. My grandmother says, 'George, teaching that child Protestant hymns!' I dip my finger in his beer to taste it. For high days I have a thimble-sized glass to drink port. My grandmother says, 'George, teaching that child to drink!' Slowly, slowly, we are pulling away from hearth and home and into the real world. My grandfather is a railway man and has been to Palestine, though not on the train. The spellings he teaches me include trick far-off towns such as Worcester and Gloucester: I cannot write, but no matter. As a grandfather, he knows the wherefores of cotton production, not just the facts of working in the mill. He knows about the American slaves and the Confederacy; also of a giant, name of Gazonka, lives on a hill outside Glossop. Grandad has ancestors, unlike us Irish people, who don't know our correct birthdays even. One of his ancestors suppressed a riot by laying low a man called Murphy, a thug at the head of a mob who was wielding a wire whip. For this feat, his ancestor was rewarded with the post of sanitary inspector.

From Liverpool he brings jelly animals and a strange kind of balloon with faces and ears, and cardboard feet you can tie on it, to make it stand up. As no one can tell me the name for this item in God's creation, I name it 'Fluke'. If you don't know a word for something, you can just ask me to supply one, but I can't blow up a balloon; I have not breath. When he's not on his shift, Grandad's always at home, he's always in his parish. My grandmother's brothers come from Hollingsworth and places even further. They give the impression, to me, of wandering the roads. They turn up unexpectedly; this is the time before telephones, or before anyone went anywhere, to be out when their relatives called. The brothers are indistinguishable elders in many woollen layers, who suck humbugs with loud slurps and sit on hard chairs with their caps still on: on hard chairs set each end of the sideboard, symmetrical, at the back of the room: as if an opera were about to burst out in front of the fireplace. My grandmother serves them a plate of ham and some Cheshire cheese. They cough long and wetly into their balled-up handkerchiefs, and even when they are not crying, their eyes seep.

When my grandmother wants her sister, she bangs on the wall. In other houses ghosts bang but here it's only Annie Connor, banging back.

The household at 56 Bankbottom lives in co-operation with the household at no. 58. Here lives, besides Annie Connor, her daughter Maggie, who is my godmother and a widow, who has a brown raincoat and a checked woollen scarf. She does errands for people and is at their beck and call. Here lives Beryl, Maggie's daughter, my heroine: a schoolgirl, dimpled and saucy. There is only one doll for which I ever care, and that one, in tribute to her, is called Beryl. She is a doll made of grubby green satin, with satin stumps for hands and feet, features inked on to a round of calico for her face, and her pointed head of grubby green satin also.

My grandfather has to be knight and commander to all these women. His possessions are a billycan, a notebook and pencil, his guard's hat and his guard's lamp. It is my ambition to be a railway guard.

In the desert my grandfather rode a camel. He

commanded it with certain words in Egyptian, known only to camels, now imparted to me.

I am three. I sit on my grandmother's knee eating sponge cake warm from the oven. The cake is pale yellow and so high that I don't know whether to bite the bottom or the top; from deep experience I understand their different tastes. We are by the fireplace, but the fire is not lit. Sun is shining. Outside the window people pass on the pavement. The back door stands open.

From hooks below the shelf hang two jugs, each of which holds one pint (though not at this moment). One is a rich cream and the other is the palest pink. They curve fatly from their lips, and the light gilds the curve: one a milk skin, one a shell. The table has fat, green, complicated legs. I go under the table to run my fingertip over their convolutions. The table's top is scrubbed white wood. The knots are like glass. I am comforted to think that next door at no. 58, our dog Rex is under the table, just like me. Peas flick from their pods into a white enamel colander, which has a rim of navy blue. The scent of inner pea pod rises around me. I count the peas. I tug the embryonic peas from the stalk, and count them as half, or quarter. My grandmother makes strawberry pie. A question people pose is, 'How many beans make five?'

I used to be Irish but I'm not sure now. My

grandmother was born on Valentine's Day, or so she always thought; my mother says that Annie Connor, being the eldest, gave out to her brothers and sisters the birthdays she thought they would like. Now some-one has produced an official paper, and Grandma's birthday's got altered to the first of March. Everyone laughs at her. She laughs too, but she's not happy to change. They say she used to be our Valentine, but now she's a Mad March Hare. Her name is Kitty, sometimes Kate; before she married she was called O'Shea. Her mother – before she married – was called Catherine Ryan. She was a small illiterate lady with an upright walk. An old person who remembers her has told my mother, 'While you are alive and walking, Catherine Ryan will be alive.' Or words to that effect.

Much later, when I'm in my teens, my godmother lets it slip that Catherine Ryan was fond of a drink. We have to revise our mental picture of this famous walk of hers, and my mother is no longer so pleased about the comparison. I defend my great-grandmother, saying that I'm not surprised if she took a drink: surely she was like the old woman who lived in a shoe, she had so many children that she didn't know what to do? Ten, eleven, twelve? I'm always losing count; there's Paddy and Martin and Daniel and Joe, there's John and Joanna and Mick. And why did her husband leave her, alone with all those babies? My mother says, it wasn't his fault; he would have come back to her, Patrick Ryan, if only she had made it possible. My mother is usually on the side of men; I'm, usually, not. Grandma says: one thing about my mammy, anyway, she may have taken a drink but she never smoked a pipe. And oh, she knew how to cook cabbage!

My mother says: 'Monday's child is fair of face, Tuesday's child is full of grace, Wednesday's child is full of woe, Thursday's child has far to go, Friday's child works hard for a living, Saturday's child is loving and giving, but the child that is born on the Sabbath day, is blithe and bonny, good and gay.'

I have various thoughts about this. I think my mother must be Monday's child. I know I am born on Sunday but it would be complacent to dwell on it. Besides, I think any parent would prefer Saturday's child. I ask, which day is my daddy? She doesn't miss a beat. I think it must be Thursday, she says, because he has to go into town every day.

My father Henry is tall and thin, with a tweed sports jacket. His black hair is slicked back with a patent solution. He wears spectacles and looks very intelligent, in my opinion. He brings home the *Manchester Evening News*.

Now Geoffrey Don't Torment Her

When he comes in from work he carries on his coat the complex city smell of smog, ink, tobacco. He has a travelling chess set, its leather cover worn, which folds up and slides into a pocket. The chessmen, red and white, fit into the boards by tiny pegs. I can play with them, but not the proper game. I am not old enough, wait till I am seven. (He might as well say, wait till you're forty-five, for all that seven means to me.) With his good pen, Henry completes the crossword puzzle in the paper. I sit on his knee while this occurs. To help him, I hold his pen, and click the ballpoint in and out, so it won't go effete and lazy between clues. I like to get close to people who are thinking, to glue myself to the warm, buzzy, sticky field of their concentration. Henry reads the racing page. It is horses who race. To aid him, I imagine the horses. He says their names. I picture them strenuously.

With my mother and my father Henry I go on the green electric train, the same colour as my raincoat; this coat I have picked specially, as blending in with the electric train; it has an industrial smell of rubber. When we step into the train, with its wide automatic doors, I take the hands of my mother and father and ensure that we all step in together, leading off with the same foot. I am afraid someone will get left behind, and I believe that once the doors have swooped closed you can't open them again. Suppose one person stepped on first, and the doors closed, and that person was on the train alone, sent ahead: worst of all, suppose that person should be me?

We go to Manchester, to Mrs Ward, my father's grandmother. (Alice, his mother, has gone up in the fire.) My great-grandfather is still alive and sitting in the back room by the range, but nobody seems to take much notice of him. He has white hair and a black suit and a watch-chain across his meagre belly; I designate him the trade of watchmaker. My Manchester great-grandmother is diminutive even by my standards, with a skull the size of an orange. She takes me upstairs and opens a chest, out of which she takes scraps of shiny, silky fabric. These are to dress my dolls, she explains. I am too polite to say I don't dress dolls, or sew with stitches.

When my mother sees the scraps, she assumes a look of scorn. Scorn is a beautiful word. He curls his bearded lip in scorn. Bastion is a beautiful world, as is citadel, vaunt and joust. Anyone who hesitates near me, these days, has to read me a chapter of 'King Arthur and the Knights of the Round Table'. I am considering adding knight errant to the profession of railway guard. Knight errant means knight wanderer, but I also think it means knight who has made a mistake. Mistakes are made all the time; it is a human thing, in a knight, to slip up once in a while.

I am waiting to change into a boy. When I am four this will occur.

*   *   *

I suppose the trips to Manchester occupied a span of
years; first the three of us went, then just myself and
Henry. I had a dread of the streets and roofscapes,
which were like a trap. I was used to looking up
and seeing hills. The bay-windowed red-brick houses
seemed to me squalid, though they were larger and
better appointed than the stone-built millworkers'
cottages in Hadfield. My cousin Geoffrey, a large
boy, was told off to take me to the park. It was
a gritty walk on the endless pavements, under the
second-hand sky, and when you arrived there was
only a rabbit of limited interest, twitching its nose
through wire. I do not remember Geoffrey's face at
all, only his huge legs in flapping flannel shorts, the
blunt bony bulk of his knees. He was my adopted
cousin, I was told; I wonder why, out of all the things
that weren't explained, this one thing was explained to
me. Back at the house Geoffrey would trap me between
items of furniture, sticking out one of those huge legs
to prevent me toddling the way I meant to go, then
when I turned back barring me with an outstretched
arm, so that I revolved about and about in a tearful
muddle. He was teasing, he meant me no harm. I saw
myself through his eyes, silly, frilly, too tiny to outwit
him or hit him, baby fists clenched in exasperation.
And this picture dismayed me, so far was it at odds
with my own image of myself. In my own mind, I
was already at least middle-aged. My judgement of

Geoffrey was that only the accident of my small size concealed my great superiority to him in every way. And this made it doubly galling, that I was stuck in an alley between armchairs, and would be rotating there until somebody noticed and said, 'Now Geoffrey don't torment her . . .'

Sitting up at the big table with a white cloth, we ate ham and tongue. The white plates were icy to the touch. Once I asked my mother, why do we always have ham and tongue? She snapped, 'Because you said you liked it.' I am amazed; I don't expect my likes to have any sway in the world, and clearly, neither does she.

The journeys home I don't remember. I expect I was pole-axed with fatigue, what between Geoffrey and the rabbit and the watchmaker and the strain on my mother's face. I left us to herd on to the train any way we could.

'Ward' means watch, it can be a place of surveillance, it can be the name for a defensible segment within a castle: a place for sentinels.

I have a friend. It is Evelyn, a Protestant. I go down the yard to play with her. Evelyn's mother is wrapped about and about in a big pinny. She is cheerful and talks in a Scottish way. My mother calls her Kath, which I think a melting name. She teaches me to say Kirkcudbrightshire. When she gives me my dinner she puts the salt already on it: Grandad has noticed that I don't take salt, but she can't know that. Her legs in thick dark stockings are the shape of bottles, so when anyone says 'Stout' I think of Evelyn's mum.

Evelyn's house – the Aldous's house – is darker than ours and has a more dumpling smell. Not being Catholics, they don't have a piano, but as they are at the end of the common yard, they have a more tidy and well-arranged plot, with flower beds. Outside our house my grandad has grubbed out a bed for nasturtiums, and trained them up a wall. He calls them storshions, and says you can pickle and eat the seeds, good in what they call a sallet, but I think, what a waste. My whole vision is filled with these pale leaves, these flowers. When I try to put names to their imperial colours, to the scarlet and striated amber, my chest seems dangerously to swell; I imagine them to be musical instruments, broadcasting stately and imperial melodies from their own hearts, because their shape is like that of gramophone horns, which I have seen in pictures. These flowers combine every virtue, the portentous groan of brass, the blackish sheen of crimson: to the eye, the crushable texture of velvet, but to the fingertip, the bruise of baby skin.

Evelyn's dad, Arthur, grows geraniums. Their

flowers are scarlet dots, their stems are bent and nodular. When Arthur comes in from work in his bib and brace, his sleeves are rolled up above his elbows, and I see the inside of his arms, the sinews and knotty veins. I think his arms are the stems of plants, that he is not human, perhaps an ogre. When I hear him at the front door I run out of the back door and run home.

I am aware, as time passes, that adults talk about this, and that it makes them laugh. He who laughs last, I think darkly. Evelyn's father has sap, not blood. If they don't know he's dangerous, so much the worse for them. Fear is nothing to be ashamed of, nor is running away, when the retreat is tactical and the enemy is a green man.

I am four. Four already! Ivy Compton-Burnett describes a child with 'an ambition to continue in his infancy,' and I have that ambition. I am fat and happy. When I am asked if I would like to give up my cot for a sweet little bed, the answer is 'no'. Every day I am busy: guarding, knight errantry, camel training. Why should I want to move on in life?

My grandfather lifts me up and sits me on his folded arms. We scan Albert Street, a cobbled road that runs at the end of our yard. Unsmiling, he nods his head across the street, to where there is a sturdy wall, higher than a man, topped with vast, flat flags, so broad an army could march on them. Its stones are black with soot, and it is a wall so stout, so formidable, that it appears it will stand for ever. He says, without emphasis, almost casually, 'Your great-grandfather built that wall.' I feel his pride, I feel the strength of his arms. I think, we built everything!

At the back of the yard is a nursery school, a prefabricated building with a plaque on it, to say that it was opened by Lady Astor; I employ someone to read it out to me. My grandfather tells me the people from the nursery hang over the back wall, saying can't Ilary come to our school? But he says, he tells me, that he wants my company, that I am too useful about the place. Grandad and I have special food, at different times from other people. When he comes off his shift he eats alone, tripe, rabbit, distinctive food that is for men. Around noon each day I take a lamb chop, and a slice of bread and butter.

Winter: we go to the pantomime. We sit high up in a box, in the dark of the afternoon. I like the box better than Mother Goose. A man wearing ordinary man's clothes comes out on to the stage. He holds up his arms. He says to the audience, 'I am Anthony Eden.' The audience roars at him. I know he is not.

*   *   *

Two problems occur. First, the spaniel. From time to time a dog would trot down the steps to our yard, look about with its tail wagging and then trot away again. It was a decrepit dog, aged and shapeless; I had been seeing it for a long time. It had a long sad face and was brown and white in patches. 'When I was young,' I said diffidently, 'I used to think that dog was a cow.' I was hoping to prompt the reply, 'Well, actually, secretly, it is,' but the reply I got was, 'Don't be silly.'

I knew it was a dog. But I couldn't help thinking that, in some way, and secretly, it was a cow. Deception seemed to be in the air. The true nature of things was frequently hidden. No one would say plainly what was what: not if they could help it.

Somehow, I got into trouble. I was supposed to have said that my friend Evelyn was a liar. She had complained to her mother Kath about it. The word 'liar', I now learned, was a terrible word, prohibited, and one such as no child might say. Even if one adult were to say it to another, it would still be a cause of scandal.

Mrs Aldous came down the yard to complain to my mother. She stood and looked stout. There were high words. My mother took me aside and spoke to me tactfully. She was trying to negotiate a formula that would suit all parties. She put it to me: 'Is it possible that you said, Evelyn, you tell lies?' I denied it. No such conversation had taken place. I was baffled. There were more high words, family to family. I stopped Kath as she was crossing the yard. I wanted to have this out. I put my hand up to detain her, and tugged at her pinny. 'I didn't say it,' I told her. She leant over me, smiling, oozing Scots sweetness, her hands spread on her thighs: 'Ahh, but lovie, you did.'

The incident fizzled out somehow. I was left with a sense of injustice and bewilderment. My friend had lied about my having said she lied. Why? Must she always be believed, and me never? I knew I had not uttered the words complained of, because I was not concerned with whether she told lies. She was a steady and regular confabulator, but what could you expect of someone with a plant for a father? I could hardly say that in my defence. It seemed like one of those knots that gets harder to untie the more you try to pull it apart.

I sensed trouble ahead. One of these days I had to go to school. My mother, who worked as the school secretary, had already brought a reading book home and tried to coax me towards it. I had taken it up secretly, and been knocked back by the 'Introduction for Teachers.' When my mother turned the pages and showed me the short squat words I would be required to master, I was simply not interested.

My grandad, when he was under arms, was an instructor in the Machine Gun Corps. He could still recite the manual, and I learnt it from him, just as, when she was a child, my mother learned it. I expect we thought it would be handy.

I spent time with my grandmother, time with her sister Annie. At no. 58, they sat by the fire on upright chairs, wooden and unforgiving; they were old, I thought, but sadly had no armchairs. They talked and talked, in an interweaving pattern of old and interesting words, and the refrain was, 'Kitty, we were born too soon. Oh, Kitty, Kitty. I wish I were ten years younger.' 'Oh Annie, we were, and so do I.' Annie Connor says she hopes she will never hate anyone, but the thing she could not fail to hate was a Black and Tan. And for people of the Orange persuasion she can't care. My grandmother simply doesn't speak on the topic. I think if a Black and Tan came to the door looking peckish, she would probably feel sorry for him and make him a strawberry pie.

At no. 56, only my grandfather occupied an armchair, his cigarette between his fingers, his brass ashtray balanced on the chair arm. Women didn't take their ease; when young, I thought, they ran about, and when old they perched on upright chairs until they died, simply slumping to the linoleum, knocking their heads on the fireplace and waiting to be carried away to the undertaker, Mr Worsley, who buried Catholics.

Now Geoffrey Don't Torment Her

Maggie, Annie Connor's daughter, was neither old nor young. She never sat down. Neither did my mother, nor my cousin Beryl. My grandmother was so creased by anxiety that her face resembled a pleated skirt. Like her elder sister's, her hands were fat, with cracked and harsh palms, and I thought she had got these from washing clothes with Fairy Soap, from wiping the fireplace with Vim. Grandma was forever on hands and knees, mopping, towing a little flat black mat she called 'me kneelin' mat'. When someone came to the door, and she didn't know who it was, she would hide on the stairs. She never went out. Officially this was because of her bad leg but I knew there were other reasons and I was sorry for them: like a child, she was too shy to speak to strangers. When something made her laugh, tears sprang out of her eyes, and she swayed on her hard chair: swayed as much as her corsets allowed, and creaked. She and Annie Connor had the most terrible corsets, salmon-pink: like the Iron Maiden, from which their heads stuck out.

My mother would tell me, later, of her parents' narrow and unimaginative nature. My grandmother had become a millworker when she was twelve years old; my mother herself was put into the mill at fourteen. She was of diminutive size and delicate health; she was pretty and clever and talented. Her school, by some clerical error, had failed to enter her for the scholarship exam that would, her parents permitting, have sent her to grammar school. But it didn't matter, she said later, because they would not have permitted. It would have been just as it was for her father, a generation earlier, for George Clement Foster pounding the cobbled streets of Glossop: *circa* 1905, he ran all the way home shouting, 'I've passed, I've passed.' But there was no money for uniform; anyway, it just wasn't what you did, go to the grammar school. You accepted your place in life. My mother would have liked to go to art school, but on Bankbottom nobody had heard of such a thing. She applied for a clerical job by competitive exam, but it went to a girl called Muriel; poor Muriel, she got all the questions wrong, my mother said, but you see her uncles had pull. Thwarted, unhappy, she stayed in the mill and earned, she said, a wage as good as a man's. The work was hard and took a painful toll on immature muscle and bone. It would be many years before the effects showed; then, with energy to spare, she danced and sang through her evenings, in amateur shows and pantomimes. Cinderella was her favourite part. Her favourite scene: the Transformation. She asked herself, could she really be the child of her parents? Or some changeling princess, dropped into Bankbottom by accident?

For the whole of my childhood I worried about the glass slipper. It is such a treacherous object to wear: splintering, and cutting the curved, tender sole of the dancing foot. The writer Emily Prager once said that she had rewritten, as a child, the second half of the story; Cinderella gets to the ball and breaks her leg. My own feelings were similar; the whole situation was too precarious, you were too dependent on irresponsible agents like pumpkins and mice, and always there was midnight, approaching, tick-tock, the minutes shaving away, the minutes before you were reduced to ashes and rags. I was relieved, as an adult, when I learned that the slipper was not of *verre*, but of *vair*: which is to say, ermine. The prince and his agents were ranging the kingdom with a tiny female organ in hand – his ideal bride, represented by her pudendum. Never mind her face: he had not raised his eyes so far. All he knew was that the fit was tight.

Three, four, I am still four: I think I will be it for ever. I sit on the back doorstep to have my picture taken. Fair hair gushes from under my bonnet. My clothes are a pair of brown corduroy trousers and a pink woolly cardigan with a zip; I call it a windjammer. I have another just the same but blue. I have a yellow knitted jacket, double breasted, that I call a Prince Charles coat. Summer comes and I have a crisp white dress with blackberries on, which shows my dimpled knees. I have a pink-and-blue frock my mother doesn't like so much, chosen by me because it's longer; people of six, I think, have longer skirts, and I am beginning to see that youth cannot last for ever, and now hope to be taken for older than I am. The onset of boyhood has been postponed, so far. But patience is a virtue with me.

We go to Blackpool to stay at Mrs Scott's boarding house, just the three of us: my mother, my father, myself. I insist that we stand before a mirror, all three. They are to pick me up and hold me between them, my fat arms across their shoulders, my hands gripping them tight. I call this picture 'All Together'; I insist on its title. I know, now, that this tableau, this charade, must have caused them a dull, deep pain. We do it time and time again, I insist on it and I am good at insisting. As a knight I am used to arranging siege warfare, the investment of major fortresses, so the reluctance and distraction of a couple of parents isn't going to stop me pulling life into the shape I want it to be.

Standing on the pier at Blackpool, I look down at the inky waves swirling. Again, the noise of nature, deeply conversational, too quick to catch; again the rushing movement, blue, deep, and far below. I look up at my mother and father. They are standing close together, talking over my head. A thought comes to me, so swift and strange that it feels like the first thought that I have ever had. It strikes with piercing intensity, like a needle in the eye. The thought is this: that I stop them from being happy. I, me, and only me. That my father will throw me down on the rocks, down into the sea. That perhaps he will not do it, but some impulse in his heart thinks he ought. For what am I, but a disposable, replaceable child? And without me they would have a chance in life.

The next thing is that I am in bed with a fever raging. My lungs are full to bursting. The water boils, frets, spumes. I am limp in the power of the current that tugs beneath the waves. To open my eyes I have to force off my eyelids the weight of water. I am trying to die and I am trying to live. I open my eyes and see my mother looking down at me. She is sitting swivelled towards me, her anxious face peering down. She has made a fence of Mrs Scott's dining chairs, their backs to my bed, and behind this barrier she sits, watching me. Her wrists, crossed, rest on the backs of the chairs; her lady's hands droop. For a minute or two I swim up from under the water: clawing. I think, how beautiful she is: Monday's child. Her face frames a question. It is never spoken. My mother has brought her own bedlinen, from home, and below my hot cheek, chafing it, is a butterfly: spreading luxuriant wings, embroidered on the pillowcase by my mother's own hand. I see it, recognise it, put out my hot fingers to fumble at its edges. If I am with this butterfly, I am not lost but found. But I can't stay. I am too hot, too sick. I feel myself taken by the current, tugged away.

*   *   *

I am changed now. Not in that fever but in one of the series, one of those that follow it, my weight of hair is cut off. What remains is like feathers, I think, like fluff. I lose my baby fat. For another twenty-five years I will be frail. In my late twenties I have a narrow ribcage, a tiny waist and a child's twig arms fuzzed with white-gold hair. At twenty-nine I am cast as a ghost in a play: as Noël Coward's Blithe Spirit, walking with noiseless slippered feet, a phantom of air and smoke. But then my life will change again, and I will find myself, like one of Candia McWilliam's characters, 'barded with a suit of fat.' I will be solid, set, grounded, grotesque: perpetually strange to myself, convoluted, mutated, and beyond the pale.

All of us can change. All of us can change for the better, at any point. I believe this, but what is certainly true is that we can be made foreign to ourselves, suddenly, by illness, accident, misadventure, or hormonal caprice. I am four, and my mother tells me this story about myself: that when I was born my hair was black and thick. At the age of five I mourn for it, weaving in my mind the ghost of a black plait that trails over my right shoulder. Once, I say to myself, I was a Red Indian. I get a feathered headdress and a tepee, bought for me in Manchester: so clear am I, about my new requirements, about my antecedents. The tepee is erected in the middle of my grandmother's floor and in it I have a small chair and small table. People step around me. I take my meals in the tepee, and believe my hands are brown, as they wield the spoon. But already it feels like a game, whereas in some previous time, in another life, I believe I had a right to this kit. I know that there is no truth in this belief. But it has created in me a complex emotion; what I feel, for the first time, is nostalgia.

It is 1957. Davy Crockett is all the go. I get a fur hat with a tail. We sing a stupid song that says Davy, Davy Crockett, is king of the wild frontier. It makes me want to laugh but I'm not sure who the joke's on. We sing he killed a bear when he was only three. Somehow I doubt it. Even I didn't do that.

Where are the knights of the Round Table? In abeyance, while I get to grips with the how the West was won. Now another thing occurs. I make a fuss! It is related to my role in life. When exactly do I become a boy?

My mother and father have been to Manchester, without me. We have brought you a present, they say, as they take off their coats. What is it? Well, it is a cottage set. It is taken out, extracted from a long cardboard box which has a cellophane window to show its contents. It is a doll's teaset, a teapot, milk jug and sugar bowl made to look like rustic cottages, with little doors and windows: though only the teapot has a roof, a thatched one. I am puzzled at first – what is the use of it or where is the amusement to be derived? Then they say, we have bought your cousin Christopher a shooting range! A shooting range? I open my mouth and bawl. Shooting range!

Well! I can hear them saying. She did make a fuss! We had to give it her!

The shooting range consisted of a metal bar on a stand, which you placed on the carpet. On the bar swung four crude animal shapes made of moulded plastic, painted in primary colours. I only remember the owl; perhaps it was the only one I recognised, or perhaps I knew that people don't shoot owls. You were supplied with a tiny rifle, which shot out a cork. You had to lie on your belly, very close, if you were going to hit the animals; you knew you had hit them if you made them swing on the bar. That was all there was to it. I found the thing tame. I had thought 'a shooting range' would entail actual destruction. Slaughter.

Everyone is disappointed. Them, because they thought I was too mature for the shooting range; and it was true, I was. And me, because I can't get to grips with this cottage set at all. They must have bought it for someone else. Some ideal daughter, that they don't have. It hangs about the house though; the teapot, unused, sits in the china cabinet, looking silly, but my mother keeps hair grips in the doll's cottage that is meant to be a sugar basin. Years pass. A dozen sets of crockery are smashed, but the cottage survives. The edges of its tiny window panes accrete a rim of grime.

And grimly, night after night, my mother studs the grips into my hair, trying to impart a curl. In time my shorn hair grows again: grey-blonde, straight, down to my waist and as flimsy as a veil. 'The weight pulls the curl out,' my mother protests. But the curl isn't ever there, and nor is the weight.

I am only playing, inside the Indian's tepee, and I know it. I have lost the warrior's body I had before the fever. My bullet-like presence, my solidity, has vanished. Ambiguity has thinned my bones, made me light and washed me out, made me speechless and made me blonde. I realise – and carry the dull knowledge inside me, heavy in my chest – that I am never going to be a boy now. I don't exactly know why. I sense that things have slid too far, from some ideal starting point.

Later, when I am six, I am given a black doll. My mother wants to bring me up to mother all races. The doll is huge, half as big as me. She cries 'mama' when you rock her: if you bother. Her tiny lips are scarlet, and they are parted to show the tip of her scarlet tongue. Her hair is close-cropped wool. She wears a white frilly dress. I know that, if I tow her about, I will make it grubby; this is a peril I have no intention of entering into. I recognise the probable expense of the doll, and that – in some way – she belongs to my mother who has procured her. Her pottery forehead is hard against my lips.

*　　*　　*

My mother and father sit together in the front room of
56 Bankbottom. It is afternoon, summer, perhaps four
o'clock; I am stupidly slow about telling the time. Certain hours bring their charged, unmistakable light, the
low rays slanting through the glass. They are sitting
with a chess board between them; not the travelling
set, for no one is going anywhere today. Black men
and white: neither makes a move. The house is quiet.
Where are the others? I don't know. I am intimate with
the chess pieces, the knight being still my favourite: his
prancing curved neck, his flaring equine muzzle. The
silence draws itself out, a long note in music; the light
glitters with dust motes. No one moves, neither man
nor woman; their hands are still, their eyes cast down.
The pieces quiver, waiting to be touched: the black and
the white, the smooth-skulled bishop, tall and powerful
Queen: the pawns, babyish and faceless. And so many
of the latter: toddling across the board, so quickly
nudged out of line and ventured, so easily picked
off by snipers, and dropped back to coffined oblivion
in the wooden box with its sliding lid. I understand
the game, almost. The groove in the bishop's head
fits the nail of my little finger, and the white pieces
are of pale wood, grain swirling around their curves;
the heads of the pawns, imagined beneath my fingertips, roll like shelled peas. Light, dust, silence; four
o'clock.

A noise rips open the air. My parents raise their

heads. It is a motorcycle, unsilenced, tearing open the afternoon, snarling down the street: 60 miles an hour. It rattles the windows; it is loud enough to wake babies, to frighten dogs. Then in an instant it has passed us, the noise fading to a snarl; changing and dying, in no time at all, to a long and melancholy drone, to a sigh. No one has spoken. But we have heard. Someone clears their throat: not me. They shift in their chairs. Their heads droop again. The racket, the roar, lasted for seconds, but the inner ear replays it and cannot help: winding away, with an afternote like vapour on the breeze, down the long and winding road.

I think, I shall remember this. I shall remember this for ever; this dying note, the slanting light, their bent heads. It is a moment of pure self-consciousness, the foretaste of what is to come. I know, besides, that they are not looking at the chess board; they are looking, covertly, at each other's faces.

I went to school, taking my knights – small, grey, plastic knights, in a bag. They were for a rainy day. My mother said this would be all right.

One had simply never seen so many children. It took me a few days to establish their complete ignorance. Evelyn I had got trained, to a degree, but no one here understood anything of the arts of war. Giant

Gazonka? They didn't know him. Machine-gunning? They simply looked blank. Suppose a camel came in, and they had to command him? They went around with their mouths hanging open and their noses running, with silver trails from nostril to top lip: with their cardigans bagging and sagging, their toes coming out of their socks, their hair matted and their bleary eyes revolving anywhere but where they should look. When they came back after dinner time, they stood in their places, beside their infant chairs, and gawped at the blackboard. Thereon was the chalked word 'Writing'. The children chorused, 'Wri-i-i-ting.' After a few days of this, I thought it would be a mercy if I varied the performance by clapping my hands and singing it, to a syncopated rhythm: *wri-ting – wri-tingg*! Mrs Simpson said, 'Do you want me to hit you with this ruler?' I made no answer to this. Obviously I didn't, but I didn't either know why she proposed it.

I kept my bounce for a week or two, my cheerful pre-school resilience; I was a small pale girl, post-Blackpool, but I had a head stuffed full of chivalric epigrams, and the self-confidence that comes from a thorough knowledge of horsemanship and swordplay. I knew, also, so many people who were old, so many people who were dead; I belonged to their company and lineage, not to this, and I began to want to rejoin them, without the interruptions now imposed. I couldn't read, but neither could any of the other children, and it was a wearisome uphill trail in the company of Dick and Dora, Dick and Dora's dog and cat, who were called Nip and Fluff, Dick and Dora's Mum-my, and Dick and Dora's gar-den. Sometimes Dad-dy put in an appearance, and if my memory serves he was balding and tweedy. It was dull stuff, all of it, and as my head was already full of words, whole sagas which I knew by heart, I was not convinced that it was necessary. Before I was entrusted with paper I was given chalk and a slate, but the slate was so old and thick and shiny that the letters slipped off as I tried to chalk them. At the end of the morning I could only show letters up to D. Mrs Simpson expressed surprise and disappointment. She didn't threaten violence. I was given plasticine to work the letters in. Instead of making them flat on the table I wanted to make them stand up, so by the time the bell rang I was, once again, only up to D. I was giving a fair impression of a child who was slow and stupid. I was both too old and too young for the place I had arrived at. My best days were behind me.

One of my difficulties was that I had not understood school was compulsory. I thought that you could just give it a try and that if you didn't like it you were free to revert to your former habits. To me, it was getting in the way of the vital assistance I gave my grandad, and wasting hours of my time every day. But then it was broken to me that you had to go; there was no

option. Not to go, my mother said, was against the law.
But what if I didn't, I asked, what would occur? She
supposed, said my mother, we would be summonsed.
I said, is that like sued? I had heard the word 'sued'.
It sounded to me like the long, stinking hiss emitted
when a tap was turned on the gas cooker, before the
match was applied. Sued, gas: the words had a lower
hiss than 'marzipan' and long after they were spoken
their trail lingered on the air, invisible, pernicious.

So there was no choice about going to St Charles
Borromeo; somehow I confused its compulsory nature
with its permanent nature. One day, I thought, my
mother would fail to collect me. She would 'forget'
and, tactfully, no one would remind her. I would be
left at school and have to live there. My grandad would
want to get me but a grandad is not in charge; he never
comes to school. Even if my mother was on her way to
retrieve me, she would be prevented by some accident,
some stroke of fate. Thinking of this, my eyes began to
leak tears which blurred my vision. Sometimes I yelled
out with exasperation and fear of abandonment. Mrs
Simpson took off her tiny gold watch, and showed it
to me. When the big hand, she said, and when the little
hand, your mother will be here. She put her watch on
her teacher's desk. The big girls and boys, who were
already five, were allowed to bring me up and show
it to me. I so hated their hands, their arms weighing
down my neck, that I tried to cry silently, but a boy

called Harry, who had blazing red hair, would call out, 'She is crying, she is crying,' whenever he saw tears dripping from my closed lids.

I thought I should be abandoned for ever, in the Palace of Silly Questions. Do you want me to hit you with this ruler?

The children's favourite game was called 'water'. At the close of each afternoon, games were given out – paper, paints, crayons – and the most favoured child of the day was called forward to the washbasin, which stood in the corner of the classroom. The pleasure of 'water' consisted of filling the basin and floating plastic ducks on it.

I got home and my handkerchief was damp. 'Did you drop it down the toilet?' my mother said. She wasn't angry, which was a relief; these days I seemed to magnetise wrath. 'No,' I said. My voice was faint. 'I had water.' How could she know the stultifying horror of those two yellow plastic ducks? Of thirty minutes in the company of said ducks? And that this was supposed to be a prize, a favour, an honour that made the children fume with envy, the unseen children at your back? Never turn your back on the enemy: any knight knows it. Worse, how could my mother think, how could she ever imagine, that I would use the school lavatories? A near-approach had been enough for me, to those stinking closets under the shadow of a high wall, the ground running from the pipes that burst every winter, the wood of their doors rotting as if a giant rat had gnawed them from the ground up. We had an outside one at home, shared with no. 54; but excuse me, *this*? I had to go to what was called 'the babies' lavatory', which was half-size. The trouble with the babies was, they were so very approximate in their arrangements; they didn't know the lavatory bowl from the floor.

So did she not know everything, my mother? I thought that was the set-up, between mother and child. I understood a fair percentage of other people's thoughts, or at least the thoughts of the people to whom I was related, the people with whom I lived on Bankbottom; I understood outlying uncles who wheezed in, and could predict with a fair degree of success what they would say next. I assumed that comprehension was reciprocal. I understood my mother to understand me. I was devastated that the mere fact of being a mile up the road meant she didn't know what was going on in the infants' classroom.

I can't say I learned nothing, at St Charles Borromeo. I learned bladder control; which is good for women, useful in later life. The second thing I learned was that I had got almost everything terribly wrong.

'Missis Simpson,' Harry called out. 'Ilary is crying again!'

*   *   *

Now Geoffrey Don't Torment Her

A strange thing occurred. My mother's hair changed colour. Once the tint of ashes, it was now a beautiful shade unknown in nature. The nearest you would come to it would be if – riding out one day in your blazoned surcoat, sword at your side, reins loose in your hands, the air mild – you observed from afar a slow fire within an autumn wood.

I may have taken some time to notice the change. Months, perhaps: functioning, as I did, on the level of the table top, and with my eyes turned inward. So peculiar was the occurrence, so estranging – so much what I would learn to call *unheimlich* – that I doubted the evidence of my senses and didn't trust my memory. When I plucked up courage, my voice faltered – 'do you, have you ... please, was your hair always that colour?' With crushing certainty, my mother answered that I should never say such a thing. My memory was at fault! I wish I hadn't made her angry, standing in the kitchen at no. 56 Bankbottom. It wasn't my wish to make her angry, in fact it was far from my mind. I just needed to know whether I could trust myself, my perceptions of things, the evidence of my senses. The answer, obviously, was no.

I had a brother. I had completely failed to notice my mother's pregnancy, though I had been besotted by her loose satin gown of peacock blue: its iridescence, its deep square neck which showed to perfection her skin's ivory glow. I went to the maternity home with my father Henry, in the shiny black car that was the Hadfield taxi, to bring the baby home. 'Wait,' Henry said: and then my mother appeared. She stood on the steps, poised, as if hovering for a photographer. She carried the shawled marvel as if it were a bag of eggs, her face tenderly downturned: on the way home to Bankbottom, I don't remember that anyone spoke. I thought it was rapture. I could have been wrong.

On a fine hot day in summer the new baby was christened. For the occasion I had a new dress, white and pale yellow, crisp as a wafer. We went up the carriage drive, beneath the grim and dripping trees, and emerged, on level ground, by the convent and the church. 'Go in,' said my mother, indicating the convent door. 'Go in, and ask Sister Joseph if she would like to come and see your brother, Ian.'

I did it. It was the only time I ever entered that building, ever crossed the threshold, and my eyes must have been so busy that they stripped the varnish from the chairs, stripped the paint from the walls: because later I would write a novel largely set in that convent. I found no one at first, no inhabited room, so I kept moving, into the innards of the place, until I found sundry nuns, perched – as it seemed to me – at high desks, in a room painted pale green. They were grey seamy nuns, with the complexions of creatures kept under stones. I thought that I must provide – in my sudden appearance, my wafer-crisp dress, and my important request – the highlight of their whiskery week, like an unlooked-for ray of grace. I said only what I had been told to say: 'Would you like to come and see my brother, Ian?'

The church was dark, at any season; dark on a blazing August day. As the christening party gathered by the font, the only reflection came from the priest's shining pate and the startling white of his robe. The infant, huge in frills, was there to abjure the devil, but his bulk was lost in his godmother's rocking arms.

My mother approached the priest, who put into her hand a lighted candle. A look of understanding, I thought, passed between them. It was a secret look, and superior to anything I could comprehend. Her demeanour was demure, smiling, yet penitential. She held up the taper and turned away from the christening party. She turned her back and walked slowly into the body of the church, away from the light. I was alarmed, baffled. I didn't know why she should be going alone, without me by her side, her protector and knight. I wanted to run after her. But only my eyes followed the candle's flicker, and followed the upright figure, enveloped by darkness, kneeling at last by the centre aisle: where she made, far from me, her own diffuse, particular light.

*   *   *

It was midwinter when my second and final brother was born. I have no memories of his christening. It is a whiteout; it is as if his first days are hidden from me, as if his first months of life are frozen in the deepest frost, inside a Russian doll with her fists sealed in her sleeves. I remember the summer that followed, when he convulsed in his pram, his tiny face blue under a blue, stormy August sky: how I put my hands on the pram's handle, rocking him, rocking him: but how he screamed, nevertheless, nevertheless, inconsolable, while the flies and bees buzzed and the storshions blowing their trumpets climbed the bamboo frames on the wall: but it was a different wall, a different house now, a different backdrop and enough to make anybody scream.

It was temper, people said, fanning their faces as his yells wound down to a whimper; it was only temper that made him howl. I thought it was being second, second boy. Or it was sleeping in our new upstairs, with its shady inhabitants; perhaps waking in the night and not knowing who was there, seeing a strange shape pass against the curtains and the street lamp. I thought it was being sent to earth in the depth of winter, and brought home swaddled to the strange house, which he had not known before he was born. God tempers the wind to the shorn lamb; this saying did not hold good, in Hadfield, Glossop, Near Manchester. By now, our lives had taken an interesting turn.

PART THREE

The Secret Garden

W hen I was a child we used to play with toys called Magic Slates. There was a coloured cardboard frame, like a picture frame, which held a rectangle of carbon paper covered by a sheet of clear plastic. You had a writing implement like a short knitting needle, with which you inscribed the plastic sheet. Behind the clear panel, your secret writing appeared; then you pulled up a cardboard tab, swished up the 'slate', and the marks vanished.

The magic slate was a favourite toy of mine. I could write anything I liked, but if someone loomed into view I could disappear it in an instant. I wrote many thoughts and observations, and letters from an imaginary me to an imaginary someone. I believed I was doing it in perfect safety. But one day the light caught the surface at a certain angle, and when I held the slate away from me and turned it I saw that the pen left marks in the plastic sheet, like the tracks of writing on water. It would have been possible, with some labour and diligence, to discover the words even after they had been erased. After that I left aside the magic slate. I didn't dare to risk it. Even now I have a horror of someone standing behind my desk and looking over my shoulder as the words appear on the screen. There is a place, a gap, a hiatus, between the hatching words, flinching and raw, and those that are ready to take their place in the world, words that are ready to stand up and fight.

If people ask my advice about writing I say, don't show your work before you're ready. They understand this, and are glad to be given permission to be cautious. I should add, don't do your work before you're ready. Just because you have an idea for a story doesn't mean you're ready to write it. You may have to creep towards it, dwell with it, grow up with it: perhaps for half your lifetime. That piece of advice – to delay, hold off – is harder to accept. The obvious question is this: how can you tell when the moment has come? I have hesitated for such a long time before beginning this narrative. For a long time I felt as if someone else were writing my life. I seemed able to create or interpret characters in fiction, but not able to create or interpret myself. About the time I reached mid-life, I began to understand why this was. The book of me was indeed being written by other people: by my parents, by the child I once was, and by my own unborn children, stretching out their ghost fingers to grab the pen. I began this writing in an attempt to seize the copyright in myself.

Perhaps I would have written it sooner if I had thought I could trust the magic slate, but after I was six or seven concealment became my habit. My thoughts remained in my head, multiplying, buzzing like bluebottles in a box.

If you stand at the end of our yard at Bankbottom, and look uphill, you can see the place where they're building the flats. They are two-storey, with pebble-dash on the outside. They are a novelty, and novelty is suspect; few people in Hadfield have thought of living without stairs. There are council houses at the upper end of the settlement, built for people from Manchester who had been displaced by the war. 'She comes from the council houses, you know,' is the phrase used; which means, roughly, lock up your spoons. I guess the council houses have superior sanitation – indoor lavatories, hot water, baths perhaps – and the Hadfield people are always anxious to sneer at anyone who they think might be going soft.

My mother lights up with indignation when she speaks of the new flats, and her incandescent hair glows around her head. 'It's scandalous! It's ridiculous! They're moving them in before the light fittings have been put up! No curtain rails between the lot of them.'

I take Evelyn down to the end of the yard. I lead her in a game, called 'Talking About the New Flats'. We put our hands on our hips. We stare furiously over the wall (the very wall where Tibby used to run, Tibby the Protestant cat). We shout, 'It's scandalous. It's ridiculous! No curtains rails between the lot of them!'

Evelyn tires of the game. She wants to play ballet school. I stay on, shouting. I wonder if, really, my mother would like one of the flats. But no Catholics can get them; that is generally known.

A few weeks on, a little girl comes to our yard and says she is from the flats and wants to play. Her name is Heather. She is pretty and respectable, but what sort of name is that? A little boy comes. He is weedy and small. He begs to play with us. How can we refuse him, Evelyn asks passionately; his age is six and three-quarters! His age does not impress me. I walk away. He runs after me and cries, and says if he can play with us he will do anything, we can hide and he will permanently seek. He will give us a penny if he can play with us: threepence. The more he raises the sum the more disdainful I appear. In the end I turn my back and walk away. Two women are standing on their back doorsteps and marvel at my hard sectarian heart. I say to Evelyn, over my shoulder, You play with him, if you want! I don't play with boys.

*   *   *

Boys are what I have to fight at school. If you can't join them, beat them. I am out of the babies' class and released from the stinking stone pen beside the latrines, out into the broad playground under the dripping trees. I come home and say, 'Grandad, a big boy hit me.' He says, 'Lovie, now I'll teach you how to fight.' He teaches fair tactics, nothing low. But when the next fight comes, I walk away with a different result. It's too easy! Punch to solar plexus, big boy folds. His head is within range. 'As you please now,' Grandad says, 'keep it easy, no need to make a fist. Try a big slap across the chops.' I do it. Tears spring from the eyes of the big boy. He reels, clutching his diaphragm, away from the railings. Oh Miss, she hit me, she hit me!

I am amazed: less by my performance, than by his; his alarming wails, his bawls. I don't want to do this again unless I have to, I decide. In only a year I will have to go to confession and learn to examine my conscience. What I am experiencing is the beginning of compunction; but is it the awakening of a sense of sin, or is it the beginning of femininity? Do boys have compunction? I don't think so. Knights errant? They have compunction for all the weak and oppressed. Shame, is somewhere among my feelings about this incident. I don't know who it belongs to: to me, or the boy I've beaten, or some ghostly, fading boy I still carry inside.

Later, when I am a big girl, ten years old, a true bully arises in our own class. He is a short boy with shorn hair, and his name is Gary, which is a bully name if ever you heard one. He is broad, white, muscled, compact, and made of rubber. He takes my beret and throws it in the ditch. I declare I will make war on him. You can't bash Gary C! the little girls say. I go after him, pale with fury, spitting with wrath. He stands his ground. I strike out. My fists sink into his torso and bounce back. The feeling is curiously soothing. I need have no conscience about him. He's made of some substance denser than flesh. I suppose he hits me back, but it doesn't hurt. By now, ten, I am disconnecting from my body. It has no capabilities and no capacities, except to be in the way, to be where it's not wanted. Gary's like a creature the knight meets in a forest, you lop its head off and it regrows. He's a monster. My breath comes hard, my heart hammers. I'm trapped in a joke with no space between the set-up and the punchline. Thud, thud, thud. 'Have you heard this one?' Thud, thud, thud. 'Two monsters are having a boxing match.'

For a while, at six, I cling to the prospect of a man's life. I play with the cleverest girl in the class, whose name is Jacqueline. Naturally she takes the name Jack, and I am Bill. The game is called 'Men' and the good thing is that even when we aren't actually playing it we can use these secret names. But Jacqueline tells me, 'You don't talk like us' and stops bothering with me. Of course I don't talk like them; they are a race of varlets, base knaves and curs. I begin bothering with the Italian children, and the ones who at home speak refugees' languages, a flax-blonde Ukrainian child and a huddle of darned and desolate Poles. I try to interest another girl in the game of Men. She is a shy, speechless child called Margaret, whose face is permanently scarlet from some inner humiliation. As her name she selects 'Walter'. It is what her father is called. I can't explain why this is no good. 'Walter', it proves, never does anything manly. The whole excitement is confined to 'Walter comes home for his tea'. So the game of Men is left off.

It is time for me to take up skipping instead. I don't want to but I have to try. I'd rather turn the rope and say the rhyme than skip. In hopscotch, another game, I should have the advantage because I have such beautiful stones to skim. One day before I was born (so my mother says) my grandmother took against the marble washstand, blaming it for being old-fashioned. She ordered it out of the house and said to my grandad, 'Smash it up, George!' Pieces of marble are still embedded in the dirt of the backyard. I dig them up and they make hopscotches that are heavy in the hand, white as a rock of sugar and smooth as ice.

Where do they go, these wonderful stones? I suppose I give them away, so that people will leave me alone. The game is better than skipping, but I find that when I try to stand on one leg, the pressure of my thoughts pushes me over.

Evelyn and I get a football and kick it at the coalsheds. She would like to be Manchester United, but I explain that Protestants can only be Manchester City. She wins, all the same; the days of playing ballet school, without me, have left her fleet-footed. But what does it profit her? She has to go to Brownies. She has to get her Darning Badge. She can't darn. She weeps in frustration just thinking about it. Evelyn has a party for her sixth birthday. There are two guests, her and me. We get overexcited and knock over our fizzy drinks: or rather, I do. Our drink is called Cyd-Apple: related to cider, but for those of a small age. I think about the glass I lost, and feel aggrieved. Later in life I drink cider, but the dry, still taste is musty, as if the glass had been kept in a cupboard for twenty years.

Overexcited is bad, fidget is bad; obedient is good. Mr and Mrs Aldous have a television set. I go down to watch the children's serial. It is *The Secret Garden.* The curtains are pulled, so the black-and-white picture stands out more; we lie on the rug, chins on our hands, like children in picture books, like illustrations of ourselves. We don't fidget at all, but I live in terror that Mr Aldous will come home before the end of the episode, will grow in from the street with his nodular, fibrous arms. At the end of many weeks I have saved up the entire story. I go home and announce it to my mother: *The Secret Garden*, here is that story. It spools out and out of my mouth, narrative, dialogue and commentary. She looks stunned. We are in the kitchen, but not the kitchen at Bankbottom. This is Brosscroft, another house entirely.

After the disappointment over the flats, my mother says, 'I'm getting us a house!' She goes to the bank for her savings. We go uphill to Brosscroft. My mother says, this is the house I have got.

There are steps up to the massive front door. Inside everything is painted in dark green. The kitchen has bare stone flags. There are gas mantles on the wall.

When I go there again, it is the day we move in. I am moving in with my mother and father and brother Ian, my younger brother being still unborn. It takes five minutes to run down the hill to Bankbottom, but still, it is a change and I am not sure I am prepared for it. The house is no longer dark-green. The front room has striped wallpaper, grey and white with a pinstripe of what we call maroon. The colour of the paintwork, my mother says, is French Beige. There is a huge old-fashioned range in the front room, but my mother says she'll soon get that knocked out. As in my grandmother's house, we will only heat one room. Hot water is got by boiling kettles. But the lavatory is our own and is not exactly outside either; it is just off a draughty stone-flagged room called 'the Glass Place', behind the kitchen. There is a private yard with a patch of grass, and high walls up which the storshions will grow. Beyond the yard is a garden. It is huge, my mother says, with the fields beyond it. When it is cleared we will be able to understand its dimensions. At the moment, the tangled bushes are head-high, when your head's as high as mine. I can't even see to the end of it.

The night we move in, the big square kitchen is a patch of light, yellow light against the chaos outside. There is chill in the air, and my mother is busy at the table, putting together a first meal. Henry, she says, the knife! It is the black-handled knife, the bread-knife, with its hair-thin blade. It has been left behind at Bankbottom; and that is *my* knife, she says.

It is true. It is the knife I am used to seeing in her hand. Henry strides out, into the blue twilight, in his black-and-white tweed coat. My mother goes to the new stove, and then peers into the dark cupboard where the gas meter is kept. The gas is turned off, she says, I will have to – No! I say. I stop her hand. I beg her. No, no, don't do it. Don't turn on the gas before my daddy comes back. Gas, sue, sue, gas, hiss, hiss, bang. I am begging and beseeching. I can't tell her my reason. Please no, wait for him, let him do it, please: it's for men. I am in the first killing crisis of my life and unable to explain how to avert it. She looks at me, a long considering look: 'All right,' she says. I am as astonished as she was, when I recited the entire Secret Garden at a stroke. All right? I take a breath. I can hardly believe any adult will take notice of me, I can scarcely believe our lives are to be saved.

I am slightly afraid that, anyway, the house will blow up; in that case, we will all explode together. But when Henry comes back, cheerful and chilled, the knife under his jacket, *alles in Ordnung.* Man switches on gas. No one sued. No one dead. No mysterious escapes, no invisible presences.

Mum pins an Elvis picture on the kitchen wall. Elvis is in his army uniform. Every day I see his fat-lipped sloe-eyed dumbness. It's not what you do, I think; you should like your husband best. I know it's all wrong, all gone wrong: and going worse, day by day.

I am beside myself with interest in the baby, Ian. I tap on the side of his pram a certain rhythm, like rudimentary code, child to child: dot-dot-dot-dot? He turns his blue eyes on me, and taps back: dash dash. Lying on his back, he kicks out the rhythm with his heels. 'This baby has almost kicked his pram through,' my mother says in horror, 'with the pounding of his great powerful feet.' When he tries to walk, I support him like an old comrade with a battlefield casualty, propping him under his armpits when he sags. His knees point outwards, his legs bow under the power of his body, and I bounce him back on course by the straps of his romper suit: 'Frog, March to the Frying Pan!' I sing. I don't know why. I have heard of it as a song, and it seems apt. I don't have any ill will towards him: only the opposite. He becomes my occupation, my hobby, my cause. I have heard of children who are jealous, I am sure that is not me. People laugh that if he falls on me he will kill me. I am a tiny doll creature with red smiling lips, stick limbs, and fair hair: an innocent abroad, a dumb broad, a feather on the breath of God.

When I am six years old I am put to bed in my parents' room at Brosscroft. So far only one bedroom of the house is habitable. The baby's cot stands against the window wall, the double bed occupies the centre of the room, my small cream-painted bed is nearest the door. I lie under a tartan rug and my fingers twist and plait its fringe; plait, untwist, plait again: the wool is rough against my fingertips. I will myself into dreaming; I think about Red Indians and about Jesus, because Jesus is a thing I am exhorted to think about and I try, I do try. I think about my tepee, my tomahawk, my stocky bay horse who is standing even now, a striped blanket thrown over his back, ready to gallop me over the plains, into the red and dusty West. Then I think about how, downstairs perhaps even at this moment, my mother is putting on her coat and picking up her bag.

I believe she will leave in the night, abandon me. We should never have come to this house; we should have stayed as we were, with Grandma and Grandad down at Bankbottom. Everything has gone wrong, so wrong that I don't know how to express it or understand it; I know that anyone who can flee disaster should do so, leaving the weak, the old and the babies behind in the wreckage. My mother is smart and fit and I think she will run, and take her chance on another life, a better life elsewhere: some princess place, where her real family lives. With her ready smiles and her glowing sunset head, she does not belong here, in these enclosing shadows: in these rooms that have filled silently with unseen, hostile observers.

My father puts the baby to bed; this hour, when he is upstairs with the baby and me, seems like the time she would run. I think that, although it will almost kill me, I can bear it if I know the moment she goes, if I hear the front door close after her. But I can't bear it if I go downstairs in the morning to a cold and empty kitchen – warmed only by Elvis, his fat face glowing like the rising sun.

So I lie awake, listening, long after my father has crept downstairs, listening by the glow of the night-light to the sounds of the house. In the morning I am too tired to get up, but I must go to school or else I will be sued. My arms and legs ache with a singing pain. The doctor says it is growing pains. One day I find I cannot breathe. The doctor says if I didn't think about breathing I'd be able to do it. Frankly, he's sick of being asked what's wrong with me. He calls me Little Miss Neverwell. I am angry. I don't like being given a name. It's too much like power over me.

Persons shouldn't name you. Rumpelstiltskin.

Jack comes to visit us. He comes for his tea. These teas seem to be separate extra meals, in the big kitchen when the lights are on and the wild gardens fade into a dark bloom. We cook strange, frivolous dishes: dip eggs suddenly into bubbling fat, so that they fizz up like sea creatures, puff into pearls with translucent whitish legs. Is Jack coming today? I ask. Oh good. I am looking for someone to marry. It's a business I want to get settled up. I hope Jack might do, though it is a pity he is not my relative. He is just someone we know.

Down at Bankbottom, they are talking about the

latest novelty from Rome: the Pope says you can marry your second cousin! That means, people say, that Ilary could marry ... if she wanted, of course ... then they turn up various names of people I haven't heard of. I wish I had heard of them: I am keen for intelligence of these candidates; I am, I already know, the kind of person who would marry back into my own family, to keep us all together, to guarantee me a supply of familiar people, great-uncles needing Cheshire cheese, great-aunts with hats discussing in low voices while wielding their spoons over bowls of tinned peaches. I have a great-uncle who was in a military prison, 'our Joe he is red-hot Labour,' my grandmother says; I have a great-aunt who for money sold her long golden hair. Why are they great-uncles and great-aunts? Where is the next generation? Where are their children? Never born, or dead as babies. Poverty, my mother says, pneumonia. I write down, 'pneumonia'. I don't know it is an illness, I think it is a cold wind that blows.

One day Jack comes for his tea and doesn't go home again. 'Is he never going home?' I say. Night falls, on this new dispensation; it falls and falls on me. In subsequent weeks I become enraged, and am thrown into the Glass Place. Jack and my mother sit in the kitchen. I jump at the kitchen window and make faces at them. They draw the curtains and laugh. I try to crash the back door, but they have bolted it.

I stamp and rage, outside in the cold. Rumpelstiltskin
is my name.

You should not judge your parents. Mostly – this is the
condition of parents – they were doing the best they
could. They were addled and penniless and couldn't
afford lawyers, they were every man's hand against
them, they were – when you do the arithmetic –
pathetically young. They couldn't see the wood for
the trees or the way through the week from Monday
to Friday. They were in love or they were enraged,
they were betrayed or bitterly, bitterly disappointed,
and just like our own generation they clutched at any
chance to make it right, to make a change, to get a
second chance: they beat off the fetters of logic and
they gathered themselves up in weakness and despair
and they spat in the eye of fate. This is what parents
do. They believe love conquers all, or why would they
have children, why would they have you? You should
not judge your parents.

When you are six, seven, you do not know this.
I feel that I myself have been judged: that I have
committed an unnamed offence: that I have been
sentenced, and that some unspecified penalty will be
exacted, at short notice. Sued, gas, sued, hiss, dead.

This is the worst time in my life: days of despair. I
am back on the pier at Blackpool, with the screaming

gulls and the wind, looking down into the boiling
sea. Words swirl over my head, words of loathing
and contempt. A great hand lifts me; it is the hand
of the law. And here is my punishment, coming now,
coming now; I feel the rush of air against my face.
The law picks me up into the wind, the law lets
me go; I fall through space, and on the rocks my
head smashes open like an egg. The sea drinks my
yellow blood.

On a Saturday morning at Brosscroft I come down
early and to my surprise Grandad is there. He is in
the stone-shelved pantry, where the air is cold even
in August. His tools are laid out there, because he's
been helping fix up the house, but now he is wiping
them and slotting them away in their canvas cradles.
'What are you doing, Grandad?' I say.

He says, 'Sweetheart, I am packing these up, and
going home.'

I walk away, my heart sinking.

In the kitchen my mother grabs me. 'What did he
say to you?'

'Nothing.'

'What?' She is burning, her cheeks flushed, her hair
a conflagration. 'Nothing? You mean he didn't speak
to you?'

I see some furious new row in the making. I answer,
without spirit, taking refuge in the literal: like the
stupid messenger, bringing the bad news twice. 'He

said what he was doing. He said, sweetheart, I am packing these up, and going home.'

Grandad walks away, down to Bankbottom, his spine unyielding, his neck stiff. Somewhere in the house a door slams. Glass trembles in its frames. Cupboards creak, the new mirror in the front room rattles its chain against its nail. The stairhead is lightless, the dead centre of the house. I think I see someone turning the corner, down the corridor to the bedroom where my father Henry now sleeps in a single bed. The walls are yellow in that room and the curtains half drawn.

What happens now? We are talked about in the street. Some rules have been broken. A darkness closes about our house. The air becomes jaundiced and clotted, and hangs in gaseous clouds over the rooms. I see them so thickly that I think I am going to bump my head on them.

Now the two boys sleep in the main bedroom, the largest in my cream bed and the smallest in his cot. I am moved into my father's room, which is the yellow room down the passage. There is no natural light in the passage, only an overhead bulb that, by casting shadows, seems to thicken the murk rather than disperse it. I never walk but run between the stairhead and my bed. Our two puppies cry in the night. They are frightened. The man who comes to paint the stairhead is frightened, but I am not supposed to overhear about that.

The door key is missing. The house is turned over for it. Every surface is checked and every drawer. The floor is crawled with padding hands and sensitive knees. All visitors – but there are not many – have their brains trounced about it and their movements thoroughly interrogated. Some two days pass, and the key returns, placed on top of the china cabinet, dead centre.

My mother stops going out to the shops. Only my godmother comes and goes between our house and Bankbottom. The children at school question me about our living arrangements, who sleeps in what bed. I don't understand why they want to know but I don't tell them anything. I hate going to school. Often I am ill with my growing pains and the breathing I am not supposed to think about and the high fever that is the same as I had in Blackpool, and raging headaches that leave me hollow-eyed. When I go back to school after a few days nobody seems to know me and behind my own back I have gone up a class. The new teacher is called Miss Porter. I don't understand how she writes down the arithmetic. I've missed something. I put up my hand and say I don't understand. She stares at me in incredulity. Don't understand? Don't understand? What broil or civil mutiny is this? Why don't I just copy from the child next to me, like all the other little sillies? 'You don't understand?' she repeats, her eyes popping with indignation. There is an outbreak of screeching giggles and adenoidal snorting.

Miss Porter is gone very soon. My ignorance remains.

Summer comes: my grandparents take me on a day trip to Blackpool. Along the promenade there are glass-walled shelters, with benches; it is in these that visitors spend most of their summers, shrinking from the wind and rain. I have no sooner set my foot on the pavements of the town than I begin to shiver and burn. My eyes close against the light and I feel as if their surfaces have been scrubbed with sand. I spend the long afternoon of a rare sunny day, stretched full length on one of the benches with my head on my grandmother's lap; my new straw basket, with its bright daisy pattern, lies useless by my side. When I get home it is discovered that I am incubating measles. A year or two later, we will go to Blackpool *en famille*, in Jack's car. That evening I will return to Brosscroft semi-conscious, the stars spinning over my head as they lift me, limp, from the back seat, and carry me up the steps to the house.

We will have our days out in Southport after that, the car deep in the sand dunes, morosely cooking chips over a primus stove.

*　　*　　*

After Miss Porter went, a person new to the school took over the class. Let us call her Mrs Stevens; she was a ginger creature with bristling hair and prominent shinbones. She was also a Protestant. This was a peculiar thing, a Protestant teacher. Someone else had to teach us catechism, which occupied the first hour of the day. It was a soft and sweet subject; on the blackboard you drew an M on top of a W, which made the shape of the wings of an angel, and was to remind you that an angel was a Mind and a Will.

What came next was much cruder. At ten o'clock Mrs Stevens charged in, bristling. She swung from her fist a big tartan shopping bag; though the tartan was, I suppose, unknown to any clan. On that first day, we were unprepared for the whirlwind that was to tear us up. Mrs Stevens didn't know our names. She didn't know our provenance. She didn't know the thing that we held in reverence, which was called Where We Are Up To. Our squared books were given out as usual. They kept our sums running carefully down the page, the faint blue lines squaring off the hundreds, the tens and the units. But Mrs Stevens didn't agree with columns. We had to work the sums horizontally, just as they were printed in our textbook. At the sight of vertical jotting, however surreptitious, she shot down the aisle and slapped you.

Mrs Stevens wrote on the board 'Problems'; and after it, a short story without a climax or moral. A man goes into a shop and buys fruit, a man fills a bucket, a man takes a train to a station to a distance of fifteen miles. A woman never did anything, you observed at once; and it wasn't a story; it wasn't a joke: it was – breathe it! – a sum. The knowledge penetrated the classroom in a low despairing hiss, spreading from the mites at the back to the one at the front. 'No talking!' cried Mrs Stevens. People began to cry. They began to knuckle their little heads. She didn't even print, but did Real Writing, which is what we called it when you joined the letters: and we weren't up to joining up! When it came to the part of the day called Reading, she expected us to follow when one child read out loud, and take up where he left off. Previously, we had thought of reading as a private activity, perhaps shared with the teacher, perhaps sweated over alone. But now it was to be communal. Communal was not much use, when some of us were up to 'Far & Wide Reader Green Book Four', while others were still mastering Letters up to D.

My first opinion of Mrs Stevens was that she was insane. My grandfather had told me that an ancestor of his had once walked the whole night, over the Derbyshire moors, with a man he later discovered to be an escaped lunatic. When I found that Mrs Stevens, who like me went home for her dinner, was in the habit of wending down Woolley Bridge Road at ten minutes past one, I would join her, and say,

'Miss, can I carry your bag?' I was interested by the way she had to force herself to smile. No anatomical operations seemed mechanical to me. I was interested by the way her shin bones went before the rest of her legs, the calf muscle flapping behind.

I suppose that, if there'd been anyone around to see, carrying her bag might have seemed sycophantic. So far as I was concerned, it was a diagnostic ploy. It had no bearing on the way she treated me, once we got back to the schoolroom: shouting and hitting. But on those journeys, she didn't talk to me; I talked to her. 'Oh yes?' she would say, and, 'Oh have you?' These minimal responses seemed correct, from her thin lips. I don't know what I told her. My thoughts on God? How to spell Worcester? God and strange spellings were my preoccupations, around that time.

There are plenty of teachers, I am sure, who pretend to like children and don't. Mrs Stevens didn't even pretend. My mother, who was interested in my progress, took a periodical called *Child Education*. Sometimes, for my benefit, she pinned up dull little pictures out of it, monochrome beside the flagrant bronze of Elvis. Mrs Stevens also had access to this magazine, and while we sat dumbfounded she read us articles out of it, about tadpoles and caterpillars. This was called Nature Study. It was good enough for grubs like us; outside, the rain hissed down on moorland and street, and small drenched things scuttled for cover, on two legs or four.

In those days – which to people born after the nineteen fifties must seem impossibly deprived and frightening, like the days of the Holy Inquisition – children were forbidden from speaking for most of the hours of the school day, unless they were asked a direct question, and thus required and indeed commanded to speak. Mrs Stevens introduced a further disability: if our hands were not employed in some specific, authorised activity, we were to sit with our arms folded behind our backs. This posture – which is as near as you can get to a natural strait-jacket – drove me to an extreme of tearful frustration. It shackled my brain and bound my hands, separated my Mind from my Will. I came home and said, *she ought not to be able to do it.* But no one can have been listening; they were listening to something else, at the time.

Soon I no longer carried her bag or walked with her down the road to school. Instead I followed her, a shadow, watching her faded ginger head bob above the collar of her coat that pretended to be fur: like a head on a platter. At first we children had talked about her, in amazed and pitiful tones; then we stopped talking. We were drawn, as a group, as a class, into a shamed secrecy, observing how she liked to drag up the boys' short trousers to slap the tops of their thighs, and pull up the girls' skirts; there was a buzz in the air which was not innocent. She would threaten us with a 'twankey,' which I thought must be some Protestant word; I understood what she meant, though. Once she shouted at a child to 'bend over,' in front of the class, and I noted how his spine became wood, and he was incapable of obeying or not obeying. She shouted the command again, then slapped him anyway.

Children were beaten, in our village, sometimes grotesquely. I was hardly out of the babies' class when on a Monday morning a little girl with a face the colour of paper whispered to me, 'On Sat'day our dad beat our Ann till she bled.' And I knew our Ann, who was, like her younger sister, a child so pallid and frail that you wouldn't think there was any blood inside her. I felt my man's spirit aroused, my ardour clenching inside my chest like a fist within a mailed glove. Saddle my charger: I'll canter up their street and decapitate him. My sword arm twitched, and I pictured one lazy, scything stroke, myself hardly breaking sweat; then the head, bouncing downhill over the cobbles. I sat shivering, my eyes closed, behind my table; I was six and the lesson was sums, the day sunny. In Hadfield, as everywhere in the history of the world, violence without justification or apology was meted out by big people to small. But there were rules. Strangers didn't hit you, only your family. Protestants didn't hit you, they had no authority over you; that was (in my mind) an established fact of life. I saw that the situation was impossible, and that, if necessary, Mrs Stevens would have to be slain.

As soon as I thought this, my fear became extreme. I trembled when she spoke to me; but what made me even more queasy than my own fear was the fear she inspired in others. I don't know if there is a case on record of a child of seven murdering a schoolteacher, but I think there ought to be, and in a way I would respect myself much more if I had done the deed; I was determined, already, to distinguish myself in my generation. But picture my situation. I am seven and becoming realistic. I know I cannot act alone. As long as a year ago, I had given up the possibility of forming a band of gallant knights, or even mustering a company of men-at-arms, to lie in wait behind the hedgerows, to swoop down between the black trees above the church.

I am seven, only seven. Fever hits me again, knocking me out of the saddle. I rise from bed each time more etiolated, my eyes paler. My hair is growing again, but I know it is always under threat when the thermometer begins to creep up the scale. To console me for being an invalid, I get 'Alice' to read. I read both her adventures but I prefer The Looking Glass. It is easy to imagine myself passing through a mirror, every cell of my body thinning, stretching, becoming transparent, forming and re-forming in some other dimension.

The three households are still divided, 56 and 58 Bankbottom against 20 Brosscroft. I come and go, eating my morning toast at Brosscroft, having my midday dinner at Bankbottom with Grandma, and at the end of the school day, swaying and fatigued, climbing the hill to have my tea in the Brosscroft kitchen, listening out for the front door, for the sound of my father Henry sliding in, for the squeak of the handbrake as Jack's car pulls up on the hill outside. No one quarrels, no one cries – only me; no words are exchanged; the situation remains unspoken, indefinite. My godmother brings the meat and the loaves, because my mother no longer goes to the butcher or the baker; she makes do with the Brosscroft corner shop, where the proprietor is kind. She no longer goes to Mass on Sunday, or indeed anywhere at all. In the evening she and Jack occupy the big kitchen, my father the front room; but mostly the men seem to time their comings and goings to miss each other. At the weekend Jack goes out and hacks savagely at the undergrowth of the garden, till he has hacked it down and the view is plain, from the Glass Place at the back of the kitchen to the crumbling back fence, to the fields beyond, and beyond the fields the rising ground of the moors. When the weather is wet, he strips off wallpaper and burns away layers of paint. He works in a fury, his sallow muscular body dripping with sweat.

But the spirits gather thickly in the half-finished

house, falling from their places in the glass-fronted cupboards to the right of the fireplace, waking and stretching from their sooty slumbers behind the demolished range. They discharge from the burnt walls in puffs, they are scraped into slivers as the old wallpaper peels away, and lie curled on the floors, mocking the bristle brush. Our daily life is hushed, driven into corners. We move in a rush between the house's safe areas, and the ones less safe, where, as you enter a room, you get the impression that someone is waiting for you. The dogs, who are no longer puppies, squeal with fear in the night. My mother comes down to them, shivering in her nightdress, and sees their hackles raised, their thin forms shrinking against the dawn light. One night, I hear my mother and Jack, discussing. I am lurking in the cold Glass Place, coming in from the lavatory. 'Well,' she says, 'so? So what do you think it is?' Her voice rises, in an equal blend of challenge, fear and scorn. 'What do you think it is? *Ghosts?*'

She has spoken my thoughts: which I thought were unspeakable. The hairs rise on the back of my neck. I do not know the word 'horripilation'. But imagine how pleased I would be, if I did.

Outside the house, what passes for life goes on. I am seven, I have reached the age of reason. Like every other little Catholic body, I must take the sacraments, penance and Holy Communion. No problem! I am great in theology.

I had begun practising as a parish priest at five years old. I used to walk with measured tread the length of the backyard, my eyes cast down, my hands folded over my heart, and I would tap sadly at Annie Connor's back door, and say, Mrs Connor, now, I've come for your confession. I believe there's something you're very sorry for, and I'm just here now to forgive you.

'Oh come in Father,' she would say. 'Would you like a chocolate biscuit?' Then, rolling her eyes in penitence, 'Oh, Father, I have been swearing!'

'Now that's very well, Mrs Connor,' I would say, 'but didn't you say the same last month?'

'I did, I did,' she would admit. 'But Father, don't be too hard, for I've a lot to make me swear.'

The doctrine of transubstantiation caused me no headache. I was not surprised to find that a round wafer was the body of Jesus Christ. I'd been saying for years that things like this occurred, if people would only notice. Spaniel and cow fused their nature, so did man and plant: look at Mr Aldous, his milky stalks for arms. Girl could change to boy: though this had not happened to me, and I knew now it never would.

When the day of Holy Communion came, I was amazed at how the body of Christ pasted itself to my front teeth and furred my hard palate. It was like eating smog. St Catherine of Siena said that when she took the host into her mouth she could feel the bones of Jesus crunching between her teeth. She must have been a very imaginative sort of nun.

It was a good thing I'd been studying for the priesthood. Otherwise, it was a great deal to take in at one go: the knowledge of the black soul wiped clean at confession, but then dirtying itself, by the mere accident of thought, by the time you were five minutes down the road from church. 'Mrs Connor,' I'd say, 'can you think of another sin?'

But then my great-aunt would reach out and grip my hands, and we'd be jumping and singing:

Oh I *met* with Napper *Tan*dy and he *took* me by
    the hand,
He said how *is* Old Ireland, and how *does* old
    Ireland stand?
It's the *most* distressful count*ree*, that ever yet
    was *seen*.
They're *hang*ing men and *wom*en for the wearing
    of the *green*.

For a long time, I thought Napper Tandy was something like a great-uncle. I thought he might show his face one day, creaking up from the bus stop and wanting a sandwich.

Once I'd got the other side of the sacraments, I found that trying to be good wore me out and frayed my temper. It involved scrupulous vigilance, over your thoughts as well as your conduct, and it went on for all the hours that you were awake and struck in again if you woke in the night. I was spiritually ambitious: sure route to failure, but I didn't know it then. I wanted an unspotted soul, a soul edged with light, like a clean but open window. It must be achieved, I thought, in calm, in stillness: as if the window opened over a blue lake, with white gulls gliding. It must be achieved among quiet people, whose speech was rare and thoughtful, whose every action was considered. I missed my grandad's methodical ways, and wished he would bring them back to Brosscroft, where the phantoms flapped and churned the air. For each task – turning mattresses, making pickles, mending a shoe – he would put on the appropriate apron, black or white canvas. He hummed as he worked, a civil hiss under his breath. He had retired from the railways, got his gold watch. It was an honourable retirement, and as an amateur pursuit he stoked the Co-op boiler; I visited him, in the shadowy underground cavern that housed it, stinking like hell's antechamber. You reached it by turning off the ordinary street and descending surprisingly few steps; but you had to know it was there, for only his authorised assistants could find the door. I didn't take hellfire seriously. I had some idea what would be the extent of the devil's coal bill.

Sometimes, of an evening, he patrolled down the road to amuse himself with the boiler at the Conservative Club, to cast an eye over its workings. He was a man in excellent standing, and as he strolled about the streets – which, unlike the rest of the family, he did freely – he met other elderly men who, breaking their own stately pace, would tip their caps to him and say, 'How dost, Judd?' Then they might cross the road, and speak of boilers they had stoked, engines that had run sweetly: machine-guns that had never jammed, thanks to the oiled ministrations of Sergeant Foster. Their voices summoned the pliant squeak of leather, the click of metal peg into its greased groove, and the dense smell of alien soil.

In a bar somewhere in the near east, Judd Foster sat down with a man called Kemal Ataturk, who told him what he meant to do for his native country. In Jerusalem, he was requested to join an ancient lodge of Freemasons: which he refused, rather shocked. He sailed into St Paul's Bay on a Sunday morning; peals of bells rang out over the waters, and as he looked up he saw the faithful hurrying to Mass, down the steep hills between the white houses. It is a sight, he said, I shall never forget. In the zoo at Cairo, he saw the rhinoceros.

Now he went about the house at Bankbottom,

subdued and orderly, and as he worked it was Catholic hymns he sang to himself: 'Mother of Christ, star of the sea, pray for the wanderer, pray for me.' In my earlier childhood, I assisted him (as he was a convert) by carrying about a big wooden crucifix that I'd found in a bedroom cupboard. 'I'm just practising, Grandad,' I'd say. 'For when I'm an altar boy and I've to carry this at Corpus Christi.'

In his religion there was Harvest Festival. Someone had told me that it was pagan. Pagans and heathens were a dubious thing altogether, condemned to a state called limbo when they passed away, together with all the little babies who died before they were baptised, of pneumonia and other causes: that cold wind that blows, that blows away salvation. It was not fair but life was not fair. Life is not bloody fair: so Jack says. Jack shouts: he feels ill used by fate. When he visited us at first, he used to stand in the kitchen at Brosscroft and play his mouth organ, leg kicking in time to the beat. He didn't regard Elvis, smirking behind him on the wall. Jack is a Protestant, or at least not a Catholic; this doesn't seem to bother my mother. In the army, he says, you had to give your religion. You couldn't say, none: if you did, they put you down as C of E.

He tells me a story while my mother combs out the tangles in my hair. His voice shakes, he is nervous. Like me, like the dogs, he is always listening, straining to catch a footstep overhead, a sound at the door. The whites of his eyes are yellowish, round the mild caramel of his pupils; he has had jaundice, my mother says. One day, when I am standing outside the front door to have my photograph taken, in my white dress for one of the Feasts of the Church, a Protestant boy across the road points and jeers at me. Jack flies across the street as if he were launched off a springboard. He is snarling, his arm drawn back, the thick edge of his hand like a hatchet. The boy backs off, holds up his hands; he runs. Jack recrosses the road, scowling, purposive; I omit to thank him. So that, I think, is what it would be like if I were Jack's little girl.

Once a year, at school and church, we had Mission Sunday, when we sang about Africans and Indians. We called them Black Babies, and collected money for them. If you did well enough with fund-raising, you were allowed to own one. You could name it: I named my baby 'Corinne', a choice found perverse and, I suspect, scrubbed out from the forms immediately I turned my back. Clare Boylan has written a novel about a Black Baby who returns in later life to look up her owner. So I won't write another: only say that during the week before Mission Sunday we sang special hymns, their tunes undistinguished but their words thrilling. 'For the infant wives and widows, Babies hurried to their graves . . .' How old did you need to be, to qualify as an infant wife? How did widowhood follow? And were the 'babies hurried to their graves' the wives themselves, or their children?

The fact is, I might have got the words wrong; I may be producing some travesty of what was on the hymn sheet. At eight, I give up hearing. Whenever anyone speaks to me I say, 'What?' While, irritated, they are repeating themselves, I gather myself, and recall to order the scattered pieces of my attention. Words are a blur to me; a moth's wing, flitting about the lamp of meaning. My own thoughts go at a different speed from that of human conversation, about two and a half times as fast, so I am always scrambling backwards through people's speech, to work out which bit of which question I am supposed to be answering. I continue my habit of covert looking, out of the corner of my eye, and take up the art of sensing through the tips of my fingers. The chess pieces now hop to my command. Henry and I sit by lamplight, in the front room of the house at Brosscroft. Babies upstairs are snorting in their sleep, my mother and Jack have gone – where? Gone dancing? I don't know. My long father sits folded into his chair, pushing wearily at a pawn; till on one inspired night, I 'castle' him, shuttling my king across two squares and bringing my rook into powerful, threatening play, grabbing the game's advantage; and he leans forward, fascinated, and says, did you know you were *allowed* to do that? The truth is between yes and no. I am eight and not such a fool as I appear. I am hardly incapable of studying the game, studying it sneakily, to confound my own daddy; though I'd prefer he thinks the move has come to me out of the blue, and I smile with dazzled surprise, as my rook, sprung from its corner, moving like a tank across country, picks off his best defenders. It is important not to try to win; to be casual; to be easy. In the same way, carelessly, he leaves his library books for me to read: his yellow-jacketed Gollancz. I read Arthur Koestler, *Reflections On Hanging*. I learn from it; I incorporate it into my dreams. I dream I have murdered someone. It is better to know about the penalty, than not.

Everybody laughs at me, because I can't hear, because I say, 'what?' My mother puts money on a horse called Mr What. It wins the Grand National.

In the days when I was still seven, after the first confession, the first communion, I walked to school down Woolley Bridge Road, with the sooty hedgerow on my left and the wall on my right, and beyond that wall the canning factory, where the slurries of unimaginable meats were processed into tins. My Guardian Angel followed, half a step behind, always and invisibly at my left shoulder. And God walked with me, I thought he did. You would imagine that I asked Him show Himself and put an end to the events at Brosscroft: the slammings of doors in the night, the great gusts of wind that roared through the rooms. But my idea of God was different. He was not a magician and should not be treated in that way; should not be asked to alter things and fix things, like some plumber or carpenter, like my grandad with his tools rolled in their canvas cradles. I had come to my own understanding of grace, the seeping channel between persons and God: the slow, green and silted canal, between a person and the god inside them. Every sense is graceful, an agent of grace: touch, smell, taste. The grace of music is not for a child who says, 'What?' My mother never plays the piano now, my father seldom; Jack is never seen to sit down to it, no doubt because he's C of E. And I can't carry a tune; I'm told brutally about this. I can't sing fa soh la tee doh without singing flat. You can pray for grace, but it is a thing that creeps in unexpectedly, like a draught. It is a thing you can't plan for. By not asking for it, you get it. For one year, I carried this knowledge, and carried a simple space for God inside me: a jagged space surrounded by light, a waiting space cut out of my solar plexus. I subsisted in this watchful waiting, a readiness. But what came wasn't God at all.

Sometimes you come to a thing you can't write. You've written everything you can think of, to stop the story getting here. You know that, technically, your prose isn't up to it. You say then, very well: at least I know my limitations. So choose simple words; go slowly. But then you are aware that readers – any kind readers who've stayed with you – are bracing themselves for some revelation of sexual abuse. That's the usual horror. Mine is more diffuse. It wrapped a strangling hand around my life, and I don't know how, or what it was.

I am seven, and I am in the yard at Brosscroft; I am playing near the house, near the back door. Something makes me look up: some shift of the light. My eyes are drawn to a spot beyond the yard, beyond its gate, in the long garden. It is, let us say, some fifty yards away, among coarse grass, weeds and bracken. I can't see anything, not exactly see: except the faintest movement, a ripple, a disturbance of the air. I can sense a spiral, a lazy buzzing swirl, like flies; but it is not flies. There is nothing to see. There is nothing to smell. There is nothing to hear. But its motion, its insolent shift, makes my stomach heave. I can sense – at the periphery, the limit of all my senses – the dimensions of the creature. It is as high as a child of two. Its depth is a foot, fifteen inches. The air stirs around it, invisibly. I am cold, and rinsed by nausea. I cannot move. I am shaking; as if pinned to the moment, I cannot wrench my gaze away. I am looking at a space occupied by nothing. It has no edges, no mass, no dimension, no shape except the formless; it moves. I beg it, stay away, stay away. Within the space of a thought it is inside me, and has set up a sick resonance within my bones and in all the cavities of my body.

I pluck my eyes away. It is like plucking them out of my head. Grace runs away from me, runs out of my body like liquid from a corpse. I move from the spot. My body weighs heavy, my feet have to be hauled up from the ground as if they were sticking in gore. I walk out of the sunlight, through the Glass Place, into the enclosed dimness of the cold kitchen. I say, Mum, I want to come in now, can I do some drawing?

I see myself through her eyes: sweat running from me, my cheeks fallen in, my chest heaving to control the thick taste of blood and sick that's in my mouth.

I pray, let her not look at me.

'Yes,' she says, sweetly, her back turned. 'Of course you can.'

It is the best yes I have ever heard. It is the best yes I have ever heard in the course of my life. If I had been sent out again, into the secret garden, I think I would have died: I think my heart would have stopped.

When I grow up I laugh at this. I say, I'm like Aunt Ada Doom, I saw something nasty in the woodshed. I say that, like Aunt Ada, I was never the same afterwards, I was always doomy after that: and what was it anyway? I don't know. Something intangible had come for me, to try its luck: some formless, borderless evil, that came to try to make me despair.

When I'm on my own, and I think about it privately, then I scarcely laugh at all.

Annie Connor dies. Not so suddenly; her chest heaves and wheezes, she takes to her bed. Though I see them at dinner time, my grandad and grandma and Aunt Annie, I would not dream of failing to call on them as I come home from school, to have a cup of tea and a bun. One afternoon I am taken up the stairs at no. 58, and as soon as I see Annie I know by the leaden, pooled blood in the veins of her face that she is dying.

I toil up the hill to Brosscroft. My mother sometimes watches for me. Just as I can't hear a straight sentence, I can't walk a straight line: she knows that the merest dot in the distance is me, if it is weaving around the pavement.

My mother's eyes scour my face. She doesn't want to be tempted down the hill to Bankbottom, if this is a false alarm; old aunts cough and wheeze, it's what they do. 'Do you think she is dying?' my mother says.

She looks into my eyes: as on the night when I told her not to switch on the gas. For the second time, she credits me with sense. She shoots down the hill. I am not with her, so I don't know what happens. But I know a kind of peace is made, between the households – or, less of a war.

It is a Saturday morning. My mother comes into my

bedroom. I have my own room now, at the back of the house, papered by Jack in pink and white. My mother says, 'Auntie Annie has gone to live with Jesus.'

I turn my face away and cry. She means it for the best, but I think it was unnecessary to phrase it like that, as if I were a six year old. Adults want you to know things, then unknow them. But knowledge doesn't go backwards. I would have understood a simple 'dead', and I can't unsee her livid, mottled face. In a way, I tell myself, it is good to have seen a dying person, and recognised her state.

I turn to the back of my catechism and find a prayer which claims it never fails. I pray it. I want my Aunt Annie and I pray that she may come back.

I know God won't deliver. He won't deliver on that sort of prayer and what I'm doing by praying it is blaspheming: kicking his godly and his god-awful shins. He didn't help me in the secret garden, and I think he couldn't anyway; I think that whatever I saw that day was more powerful than any bewhiskered prayer-book God, simpering in a white robe: his holy palms held apart, as if he were sizing up a plank. Why didn't he try, though? He could have done something. He could have showed willing. I wanted him to manifest, and own me, take charge. But he never turned up, in the secret garden; the old bugger never got out of bed. Now, a graceless being, abandoned, I pray silly stuff to spite Him. You have these so-called prayers that always work; on the other hand, you know that the past can't be recalled. Time doesn't flow backwards; all the scientists say so.

Soon afterwards, leaving school at twelve o'clock, I hurtle straight downhill, down the carriage drive and across the road. It is a main road, and the carriage drive comes out on a straight run between two deep bends. But there is little traffic, none of it fast: who would need to speed towards Hadfield?

I escape by inches. I look back, to the long black car that has squealed to a halt; I shudder once, and bolt for home.

Big girls have turned back; they are screaming. They pounce on me, as I try to zigzag past them; I want to run up the road to Bankbottom, but they won't let me. I go rigid; they half lift me and drag me back towards the scene of the incident, my heels scraping the ground. The driver has put his window down, and is leaning out of it. He is a man with a bald dome, sleek wings of hair at the sides of his head. My own head is ducked by a big girl's palm, and my face is thrust towards his; he wants to see me, they want to exhibit me. He is shaking. Did you not see me, he says? He is not angry, but guilty, aghast; he is a stranger. His fingers are curling around the wheel to control their quiver. Did you not see me? I pity him.

There is cold sweat on his forehead, like the sweat of death.

I am tugging to be away. My child compeers are gathered – well, trust them to be in on a drama! Others are pouring down the drive, so are teachers and nuns. Two big girls have me by the wrists, and are trying to persuade me back up the drive to the school. In silence I pull away from them, teeth clenched. I pull, they pull, till I am in danger of being divided, like the child in the judgement of Solomon. They are fifteen years old, with great brawny arms, with the woody scent of motherhood rushing from their pores and enveloping me. I make a plot, I devise a ploy; I allow myself to be drawn forward, sweetly, then I spring into the air and hurl myself backwards to the length of my arms. Their grips yield: I run. All I want to is run: to 56 Bankbottom, to my grandma. Inside I'm howling with rage. I'm alive, what's the problem? What's new? I live and die by inches.

My grandma is giving me beans on toast. She sinks on one knee to toast the bread before the fire. I love this meal; but today it dries in my throat. I cannot swallow. Her puzzled face swims after me as I creep back to school for the afternoon.

Next day – it takes time for the news to reach her – comes the rant from Mrs Stevens. I am shouted at and held up as an example of a person nearly dead, nearly dead by my own ignorant self-willed dashing.

And what do they say at home, what do they have to say about it all, hm, hm? I sit in a sullen, snarling silence. My 'best friend' Bernadette raises her hand and says, 'Miss, she's not told 'em.'

Not told 'em? What? Not carried home to my grandmother the news that I am just a foot or eighteen inches from being ground into the tarmacadam, my arms fluttering and my neck snapped like a pigeon's? A long 'aw–hh' from the class is shouted down by Mrs Stevens. Now I am accused of being a deceiver, as well as nearly dead. My 'best friend' whispers that I'll have to tell it in confession: it's worse than a lie, she says. And before the week is out, a distant relative, seldom seen, turns up at Bankbottom with a highly-coloured account of the occasion: the screech of tyres, the burnt rubber on the road, the cry of nuns, the pre-emptive tolling of church bells.

This is a child's life. You have no rights, over your life or death. Every event that happens to you is appropriated by others, who think they know better than you do what is going on in your head. So don't speak, even under threat, especially under threat; don't feed them information they can use against you. In the court of public opinion you're sentenced: toll the dead bell.

I have my own courtroom, my own trial. A noose for Mrs Stevens. A noose for my distant relative. A noose for my 'best friend'. A noose for Mother

Malachy, headmistress of my school, who stood at the gate, gloating over the drama, and propelled those great girls down the drive to tear me apart. But grace for the driver. Grace for the great girls. Grace for me, running; grace for my sealed lips; for my grandma, kneeling before the fire. Except there's no point in praying for grace or asking for it any more, since God is obviously looking but not looking in my direction.

Now that Grandad was retired, he had more time for testing me on spellings. First every day he oversaw my dinner, indulging me – take that piece of the loaf, it is what you prefer. Let's see you eat this cake; this kind of cake is what we call a Savoy. My sad and nauseous days gave him the more excuse for ingenuity, carving an apple into slices and laying it out on a plate, tempting and sugared.

But a day came when he felt his age, and mine too, and then he led me up the steep stair to the garret, a room whistling with cold. There were white planks underfoot, and standing in the middle of the room, under the skylight, was a rabbit hutch. And in it were books.

Their pages were crisp and sallow, nibbled at the edges by time, or perhaps by rabbits. Their covers, once green, burgundy and navy blue, now inclined to the condition of black, so ancient and tarry that

I thought it would come off on my fingers: not that I gave a bugger, excuse me Father for swearing. I wanted books like a vampire wants blood. My daddy Henry took me to the Hadfield library, where there was one bookcase for children, and I had read it upside down and inside out. I had read the books so hard that when I gave them back the print was faint and grey with exhaustion, and I thought that one day the librarian would notice how I had been depleting them and tear my ticket up.

My own bedroom at Brosscroft was a room where the sun shone, the only room in the house in which you were safe to put anything down without it being sucked into phantom-land. Such books as we had were dumped there. Some had come to Jack in the course of his life: a set of yarns called *Out with Romany*, country lore and country life. Looking into it made me ask, was Hadfield the country, or the town? It seemed to occupy some no man's land, some place not well-defined in any book. There were very few streets, but very few trees. There was moorland, dappled with snow in April; there were no birds, except for the sparrows and starlings, which women fed with the crumbs ground from the heels of loaves.

I read Romany; I learned to love the hedgehog, and the ways of sneaky fox. I read the horrible, foxed, mouldy volume of Tennyson, someone's Sunday

School prize: Mariana in the moated grange. I read
Steps to Literature: Book Five. It was a small book, its
pages yellow and decaying, its greasy cover stamped
with the word 'Specimen'. Look inside: the subtitle was
'Readings on Europe'. It was a book of extracts. I read
them all.

In a certain village in La Mancha, there lived not
long ago one of those old-fashioned gentlemen . . .

It is now sixteen or seventeen years since I
saw the Queen of France, then the dauphiness,
at Versailles . . .

Once she did hold the gorgeous East in fee . . .

I have sat for hours at my window inhaling
the sweetness of the garden, and musing on
the chequered fortunes of those whose history
is dimly shadowed out in the elegant memorials
around . . .

I am mad about this book. Like Washington Irving
at the Alhambra, I issue forth at midnight to get it.
I wake up before dawn to read its single scene from
Julius Caesar: the scene where Antony pitches the mob
against Brutus. The scene is prefaced by an extract
from Plutarch, so I am keyed in on the storyline. I
like the story, all of it: the violence, the polemic. I
wish I had written it myself. Brutus, of course, was in
the right. Antony had the best use of words. Beware

words; beware the slick. 'If you have tears . . .' Beware the sentimental crowd.

So this, I think, is the complete works of Shakespeare, a thing which I have heard people mention. In my opinion, it deserves all the applause people heap on it. I learn the death of Caesar by heart. I murmur it, in times of stress, as the pious murmur the rosary. One day, my breath held, hurrying, I go down into the yellow room, my old bedroom shared with my father. I look in the drawer of the little cabinet beside his bed. There I find my book of tales of King Arthur, which has been missing for as long as I can remember. I am overjoyed. I fall back into the stories. I now like the ones I used to miss out. I like the Grail. I imagine how the knight lies rigid in his bed while the chalice, half hidden in its veils and airy wrappings, glides slowly across his field of vision. In the back bedroom of my grandmother's house at Bankbottom − my mother's old bedroom, an empty room where I am allowed to play − I have sometimes seen similar shadows, objects that are unnameable, that float and are not solid, objects through which the wall behind them can be glimpsed. They seem to me domestic things, plates and cups, bowls: as if they were echoes or shadows of the objects in daily use in the kitchen below. In time I realise that anything in this room can become translucent. I spend a great deal of time there, mostly alone, pursuing no particular game, just being. Sometimes my friend Evelyn comes to play. We peddle backwards on an old child's bicycle that leans by the wall. My grandmother labours up the stairs with our favourite meal of banana sandwiches. The room, when Evelyn is in it, is entirely solid.

Winter: it is dark by half past four, and the curtains are drawn in the front room at Brosscroft. The evening is silent; Jack has gone to night school, my father Henry is somewhere else, at the jazz club or the library. By the light of the low-slumbering fire the brothers are undressed, and taken upstairs to bed. Their clothes come off in three effortful tugs, from their shoes and socks upwards. It is my task to pick up after them, to strip vest from teeshirt and turn the arms of their jerseys the right way out: then uncrease and smooth them, spread them out to life size, as if I were making little boys from wool. I shake out their tiny socks from their scattered shoes, line up the four shoes in pairs, then put everything tidily away in a deep drawer by the fireside. Sometimes when they have gone, I sit gently on their rocking horse, which is really a springing horse, which bounces on a metal frame; I am too old for this toy, and the thought that I might be seen riding it brings a blush to my cheeks.

I am nine; knight errantry is behind me, and my progress is complete, from hero to zero. I am going to become a woman, though I cannot imagine of what sort. A little girl, flat-chested, can't imagine her body will ever change. One days she becomes conscious of the brushing of her blouse against her skin. She puts her fingers there – I do – and feels enraged at the thought of what is to come. The whole process is beyond control. You have no choice in it. My body is getting the better of me, though people seem to feel I am responsible for what it does. My small blood vessels are unstable; I blush if anyone speaks to me, if anyone looks at me. I can't help this, but it seems to drive my mother and Jack into a frenzy of irritation.

I listen; above I hear ponderous footsteps, I know the boys are not in bed yet. Cautiously, I let out my breath; I let the horse spring beneath me; I trot it for a quarter of a mile. My fingers brush its reins and bridle, most unconvincingly rendered in painted metal. I raise my eyes, and they rest on the drawn curtains of our front room at no. 20 Brosscroft. Against a background of silver grey, the curtains have a repeating design of – windows.

They are Mediterranean windows, with gay blinds and plants spilling from pots and wrought-iron baskets. I appraise them; my cold northern soul flips in my chest. I want to live behind those windows and to be warm. There are two patterns of window, one rectangular and one arched, and I can't choose between them; the rectangle is more elegant, the arch more enticing.

At 20 Brosscroft, firelight gutters, draughts suck at the flames, the Glass Place rattles, the garden yields up its dead secrets. But at the Alhambra, as *Steps to Literature* assures me, 'the garden beneath my window is gently lighted up, the orange and citron trees are tipped with silver, the fountains sparkle in the moonbeams, and even the blush of the rose is faintly visible.' I imagine my life behind those windows, the texture of my life: I carry the sun inside me as I move through the shaded, scent-drenched rooms.

Many years later, I asked my mother if she remembered the Brosscroft curtains, the curtains with the window design. I used to imagine, I said, that I vanished into their texture and lived there, within the warp and weft of their design, that I lived behind their shutters and balconies, that I owned those window boxes and those pots with the spilling scarlet flowers. My mother turned away, so that I couldn't see her face. She whispered, and I, oh so did I.

Those were cold years for her. Love doesn't light the meagre fire in the grate or fill the children's bellies. And childhood was a sort of gulag for me; I was cut off, adrift. Conditions changed from year to year; sometimes I moved to another camp, where I waited to see if the regime would be better or worse, more or less survivable, and where I scrambled quickly to learn the rules. It wasn't particularly anyone's fault. Few people acted with malice towards me. It was just that I was unsuited to being a child.

At ten, I developed catastrophic hay fever. I sneezed and shook for a whole summer long, my weeping eyes were blind and sealed to slits. Between my eyelids I saw flashes of scarlet, the petals of flowers: geraniums.

When the day of the Eleven Plus results came, I was at home as usual, sick. I had no expectation that I would earn a grammar school place, and no particular hope of it. It seemed out of my hands – as it had been for grandad, whose parents couldn't afford the uniform: as it had been for my mother, whose teachers had simply forgotten to enter her for the exam.

Just after four o'clock Bernadette came to the door. I went to open it. She stood squarely on the front step and looked me up and down. 'Ye've passed,' she said, unsmiling.

I fell back into the house, my hands across my heart. And you?

Soberly, she nodded. Perhaps she was in shock.

'Give Bernadette some orange juice,' my mother said.

I went into the dim pantry with the deep stone shelves. The ghosts rolled under them, sucking their teeth in envy and malice. My hand trembled, the neck of the bottle knocked against the rim of the glass.

Passed. Who would have thought it? Passed. So I can have a life, I thought.

Within a few weeks we were moving house: myself, not my father, my mother, Jack, the two little brothers and the one dog that was left. By the end of the summer we would be gone. We would be gone to another town. We would have a semi-detached house. It would have a lawn. It would have a rockery; it would have an apple tree, and 'even the blush of the rose is faintly visible'. We would have new carpets and another name. We would be gone so fast that by September, when the new school year began, we would be a scorched trail on the air.

My childhood ended so, in the autumn of 1963; the past and the future equally obscured by the smoke from my mother's burning boats.

PART FOUR

Smile

For the next seven years, I lived with my mother and Jack, two brothers and a dog, in a house in a small town in Cheshire.

Sometimes, when I had known Jack at first, he would lend me his fountain pen. The pen's name was written on its barrel: Swann. When I wielded Swann, my writing came out mysteriously like his, black and small and without ornament: a man's hand. But by the time I reached my teenage years, this privilege was withdrawn. I had to hack my own words on to paper with whatever deficient instrument came to hand. My handwriting was always changing, getting remodelled; my practical skills were not many, and those I had were hardly commercial. By the time he was midway through his teens, my brother who had kicked the bottom out of his pram could rip an engine out of a car, and practically build a house; at the same age I couldn't even wire a plug. I lived in terror that Jack would one day teach me how; but he didn't seem to think that women and electricity could be trusted together. Luckily for me, we had moved to a house where there was no gas.

When you go to a new country, or join a new tribe, the first thing you must learn is the ceremonies of greeting and farewell. In our new town – or 'village', as it called itself, looking back steadfastly to the genteel past – the easy familiarities of Hadfield were nowhere in evidence. No one went from house to house with the gossip, or barged into your front room yelling, 'It's me.' People had bells on their doors, and those bells were for use. When people asked, 'And how are you?' it was not a question that demanded a reply. When you left a shop, instead of Hadfield's downbeat 't'rah', they sang out, 'Bye now!' Even men sang it; it didn't sound very manly. In Hadfield, men had no form of farewell that I could remember. If they were going out, why should they mention it? It wasn't your business. They simply wrenched open the door and hurled themselves, teeth gritted, into the moorland wind.

Our new house was on an avenue, not a street. It had a glass porch and a bay window, a hall, two rooms, a small poky kitchen: upstairs, two good bedrooms and a box room – mine – and a bathroom. A bathroom! Before we moved in we used to visit the house, for fixing-up sessions. The empty rooms smelled of floorboards. The little boys played in the garden, among the late summer ghosts of the hybrid teas. Secretly, upstairs by myself, I climbed into the bath without any water, with my clothes and shoes on, to see what kind of enclosure it was: where your head came, and where your feet. 'It seems strange', I said to my mother dreamily, 'to say you've never had a bath before.' She looked at me in shrinking horror, as if she feared I might say that outside the house.

The bathroom was old-fashioned, and the first thing Jack did was to box the bath in so that you could not see its legs. Later he made the panelled doors flush; everything was being squared up, modernised. My mother fixed a panel of black quilted plastic to the back of the sitting-room door, and secured it with shiny brass tacks. It was *le dernier cri.* None of the neighbours had such ideas about décor. Their houses, glimpsed but seldom entered, had patterned carpets and chintz; their pale wallpaper had flowers on, and there were lace mats on their sideboards. My mother was too go-ahead for a sideboard.

But there were some markers of the middle classes we could not do without. We went out to buy a three-piece suite. It was boxy and angular, moss-green with seat cushions of a dashing bold check; it was nothing like the suites of the neighbours. And those curtains that came only to the windowsill, my mother said, she powerfully despised. Our curtains with the windows on were left behind at Brosscroft; our new curtains had dramatic silk stripes and fell to the carpet. When they were drawn, shutting out the autumnal garden, the scrubby lawn littered with windfalls, the creaking pergola arch with the rotting wood and the rambling rose, I whispered to my mother, 'It's like a stage.' She smiled, gratified. Behind the curtains night fell, peaceful on ornamental stonework, on dwarf conifers and garden ponds; the drama was played out among us, the audience. Our house was like a million other houses in a million other streets, but our perplexities, our hesitations, were all our own; we had secrets, and we did not think other households harboured any.

But I must have begun to know that every house was different, that every house had a secret life, because at the end of the summer of '63, after we moved into the avenue, I got into the habit of walking up and down, examining the façades of our neighbours, eyeing up their paintwork and scrutinising their shrubs. Then I went further afield, up the avenues, drives and closes and around the crescents, noting how some houses had square bays and some had portholes for porch windows, some had panes of stained glass and some had scrolly metalwork gates instead of plain wood. Some houses had names. Ours was called 'Arcadia'. But the name had dropped off long ago, and it had become plain Number Four.

One day, a week or so before we moved in, I walked into an empty room and saw Jack's tweed jacket hanging from the doorknob. It surprised me; empty clothes have always been worrying to me, and it was as if Jack himself, being occupied elsewhere, had left the coat *in loco parentis*, imbued with his authority and power. The boys were outside, my mother and Jack were upstairs; I was alone. Sunshine spilled in at the uncurtained window. It was afternoon: that time, around three o'clock, when a day seems to pause and yawn, before stretching itself and ambling forward towards teatime. It was August; the air was still; there was no noise, from garden or street, neither car engine nor birdsong. I walked across to the jacket; I watched it for a moment, then touched its rough tweed. I stood for a time, my fingertips brushing it lightly. Then I put my face into it and breathed in the complex scents that collected in those days in fabrics: industrial smells of metal and rubber, rural smells of ordure and woodsmoke: the smoke of other people's cigarettes, the Cheshire smell of grass clippings, the lingering Derbyshire smell of peat. I felt a spasm of grief, as if Jack were dead, and as if his soul had gone into the weave of the cloth.

My grief may have been self-serving. Must have been, really. He was all we had now for a husband and a father, even though he was neither of these, and my mother didn't cease to remind me that not many men would have done what he did, take a family on. But why did she say this? It didn't make sense to me. I was determined not to be grateful for what was simply inevitable; it was like thanking somebody for the fact that it's Friday, or complimenting them on having a nose on their face. How could Jack have got her, without us? It wasn't possible. It wouldn't have worked. My mother was a jewel and her sons were her setting; I was her packaging material, to be ripped through in excitement and tossed away. So I felt. The boys could grow up and be Jack's, or as good as: men want sons. Nobody wants a skinny ten-year-old girl with sticky-out teeth and a habit of flinching when you speak to her: a girl who will soon be bleeding all over the bathroom at monthly intervals, whose stockings will always be laddered and whose fingers will always be inky, a thing not childlike, not womanly, always remembering, always knowing things.

When I went to my convent school at first I didn't know much. My last years at primary school had been conducted under the eye of Mother Malachy, which had rolled at me around the curve of her starched headdress.

Many a dreary afternoon I would contemplate her, as she stood at the head of the class and prosed on about this or that. I studied her so that, when I was out of her presence, I could draw her, commit her to paper: my eye traced the bulb of her nose, the coarse swag of her chin. They were long, those days, those schooldays, and Malachy was a heavy static presence within them, her profile unyielding against the cold rainy light. At eleven years old, I knew, you failed your scholarship exam and moved on, to a new school for Catholic failures that had been built in Glossop; until recently, the failures had stayed at St Charles and rotted, under Malachy's rule, until they reached the school-leaving age. I thought I would never attain this failure; the days stretched themselves out, arithmetic in the morning out of the brown book, then a subject called Intelligence, then English out of the green book. *General Progress Papers*, the books were called, and they had gaps to fill in, where, with a blunt failing pencil, you tried to impose your version over the wrong answers of the people who had gone before, battling away against all the years of folly and error which – if you turned up the page and fingered the back of it – you could read like braille. I thought that time had stopped for me; I thought I should never be free of Malachy, never reach the age of eleven; I felt that she had absorbed me, drawn me to her by my woolly cardigan, by means of static electricity: drawn me into the fusty depth of her habit, and then leached me into her thick body, as if she were my mother indeed, and I was beating at the walls of her nunly womb. The lights burned all day in Hadfield winters, the great radiators puffed and fumed and stank, the odour of wellington boots and nit lotion and nun became so thick you felt you could graze it with your knuckles; you were, very often, spoiling for a fight.

Malachy's idea of education was to use up a whole half-hour by going around the class, asking the same daft question. In Lent, she said, the statues in church are draped with cloths, velvet cloths of purple black: did we all know that? Yes, Mother Malachy, we chorused: well, they did, I never chorused anything. So; she said to each child, *how* do you know that? After a prolonged, nervous hesitation – Mother Malachy was very violent – the first child had a happy inspiration. 'My mother told me, Mother Malachy.' Next child: 'My mother told me, Mother Malachy.' Halfway through – we'd have been, I suppose, thirty-five in the class – some exasperated hero broke out, 'I remember it from last year, Mother Malachy.' Shock rippled through the room. The rhythm was broken. But after another excruciating hesitation, the next child resumed, 'My mother told me, Mother Malachy.'

But when my turn came, I said nothing. Not a word would I yield. I had made a policy: I would answer reasonable questions, but not ones I thought were senseless. I would write the answer to any question, but speaking was different. Talking was forbidden to pupils in class. If the rule of silence had been imposed, I too could employ silence. Why should I speak because an arbitrary decision had been made, that it was the time for speech?

'Intransigence' was not a word I knew. But I was learning from my mother, learning to keep intact my own opinion of myself. I was learning it too early, though, for my circumstances. My adult reasoning and my small status were at odds. One day Mother Malachy hit me so hard on the side of the head that she propelled me across the room, and spun around my head on the stalk of my neck. Ho, fisticuffs, Madam! I said to myself. I put a smile on my face and turned my head the right way round again. I was eight then; by the time I was ten, my contempt for her was so complete that I must have worn it like armour, for she never exerted herself to lay a finger on me. I was amazed, of course, when Bernadette came to the house, four o'clock on a spring afternoon, to tell me that we weren't going to Glossop to the school for Catholic failures; that we had passed our examination and were going, instead, to the Convent of the Nativity. I was still more amazed when I got there, and found that the nuns didn't punch you; not even the lay-teachers seemed to want to go ten rounds with a six-stone opponent.

My convent school was a small, gentle institution, a little bit snobbish. Because it was considered the 'good' school of the area, the Protestant burgesses of the district paid fees for their daughters to go there, in the knowledge that their girls would be turned out well-spoken, polite and poised. The sheer numbers of Protestants per class shielded us from the worst excesses of religious zeal. Convent girls, of course, like to consider themselves as restricted, trammelled and oppressed. So the actual conditions prevailing – which I thought quite liberal – did not prevent the girls telling each other in tones of shocked mirth those stories that are always current in covent schools: that Sister So-and-So had said – 'to my elder sister', or 'ten years ago' – that the Holy Virgin would never have sat on a boy's knee without putting a telephone directory under her thighs, or that Our Mother Mary would never have worn patent leather shoes in case they reflected her knickers. Mother Mary need not have troubled about the footwear; you would have seen nothing even if we'd walked over mirrors, because our maiden crotches were hugged tight by navy blue garments so thick and dense that they could with profit have been worn by men off to the Antarctic. My first set of knickers self-destructed in the course of time; how can this be, were they carried off by giant crows, or did someone throw acid on them as they hung on the washing line? I never got any new ones, so I was forced to rummage in our airing cupboard for whatever was around by way of shrunken nylon panties; and so for many years, and even when in course of time I was elected Head Girl, I slunk around with an illicit bottom.

The Convent of the Nativity, at first, had been off limits to Hadfield girls, to Derbyshire girls in general. Any girl who sneaked under the wire and wasn't a Catholic failure was expected to get on the train to Manchester and take herself to one of the gaunt, sooty sanctity factories that ground the girls of the north-west into the pious paste of Catholic womanhood, that turned out Catholic mothers, Catholic nurses, Catholic teachers, all of them with an eye cocked for a good Catholic boy with whom they could collaborate to produce a new Catholic generation who could be ground in the same way. But this was of no interest to my mother. She wanted a bit of class.

The education authority said there was no debate about it; they wouldn't pay for Derbyshire girls to go to schools in Cheshire. They had made their arrangement with the Manchester schools, to accommodate the left-footers, the papists, the awkward squad; they weren't going to vary it. But my mother had set her heart on this school for me, and she and Jack – since they had to run somewhere – ran over the border and into the small town where the convent was situated. In that way, the problem was solved; but my mother, with pluck and verve, fought the battle with the education authority on behalf of those other little girls left behind. She did not believe in the Manchester convent schools; they were unfit establishments. The girls stole from each other, she said, their conduct and language were shocking; they had ground my cousin Beryl, and ground her into a good Catholic shorthand-typist. My mother envisaged something grander for me; and why shouldn't Hadfield girls have their chance? She'd had none; but she would make her name, battling this issue, she'd show she was a force to be reckoned with. Eventually a compromise was cobbled together, and on the first day of term, September 1963, a small glum band of Hadfield lasses stood on the edge of their posh new world. In retrospect, this was unfortunate for me. I had changed my surname to Jack's, and was pretending he was married to my mother, and that I was his daughter. I had to go on and on pretending it. The lasses knew better. They might be only eleven but they weren't complete idiots; otherwise, they'd have been Catholic failures, wouldn't they? Word spread.

For a while, the posh girls at the convent laughed at me: as much for my accent as because they heard rumours about my private life. There was an attempt, rather feeble, to bully me: thefts of my possessions, pages ripped out of my books by unseen hands. People say girls can be cruel, but it's nothing a smart slap on the jaw won't cure. Strangely, though, I didn't have to get violent at all. One day in the lunch hour, when the whole school, rain or shine, was turned out of doors for fresh air, I saw our Top Nun walking alone, on an eminence, a raised patch of ground; she was a tiny, fierce item, horribly feared – though I did not know it – by parents and pupils both; after Malachy, she seemed to me a pussy cat. On New Parents' Day, we had been treated, mother and child, to a good thrash through the school rules and sumptuary laws; all uniform to be purchased from approved stockist, no hand-knitted or self-contrived items, no jewellery except holy medals, and no nail varnish or cosmetic adornment on pain of torture and death. After this telling-off, my mother had approached the Top Nun, strung-up, somewhat subdued. She was worried that I was not physically robust, that I would be found wanting: she was afraid I was not plain enough, worried that my streak of ashy hair, which once again fell to my waist, would be flouting the rules against conventual simplicity. Seeing a mother heaving in view, a parent with the temerity to make an individual approach – a parent who had been told but not told hard enough – Sister gave a pained, ironic smile.

My mother indicated me. 'She can't do games,' she said, 'or P.E. The doctor . . .'

Sister looked me over, where I shrank at my mother's elbow. 'Gym?' she said mildly. 'Well, we do find most girls are very unhappy if anything interrupts their gym.'

My mother nodded and nodded, sacrificing me within seconds on the altar of Most Girls: my colics and cramps, my pains and my panics. Then she burst out with her real, eager, zealot's question: 'Long hair – is that all right. Shall I have her hair cut off?'

Sister Mary Francis stared at her for a moment; then gave a sweet giggle, like a little girl's. It was a sound I would wait many years to hear again. Oh heavens, she said. Oh, no, don't do that. That will be *quite all right.* Tied back, you know. Navy ribbon, if you must. Oh heavens ... don't cut off her hair.

We were held in a moment – my mother and I – of blushing embarrassment. Perhaps only I blushed; my mother was a woman, and had face. And I imagined Sister, that night, going back to the company of her fellow nuns, putting her feet up, rolling her eyes, and exclaiming, 'New parents! What *are* they like?'

So now, this misty November lunchtime, sorry for her solitary state, I approached her, and got chatting. Arrival at the convent had reduced me, once again, to a very little girl, a starter, with simple easy manners; hierarchies were never obvious to me, and I felt warmly towards this tiny Top Nun whose nose and lips were blue from cold. Had she not defended my hair? For two pins, my mother would have cropped my head, and sent me out looking like a convict; the girls would have said I had nits, if – at the Convent of the Nativity – they knew what nits were, and in any case the loss of my hair would have taken away my only distinction. I may – though I don't remember this clearly – have taken Top Nun's tiny poisoned hand in mine.

'Hilary,' she said. (Top Nun aspirated.)

'Yes,' I said; we chatted a while. Was I managing the gym, she asked? Not really, I said, I was generally rather poor at hopping and frog-jumps, but I was resigned to it. 'However, while very happy generally, I have a complaint. Amongst other items, my shoe bag has vanished. My shoes in it.'

'Have you had a good look for it?' Top Nun said.

'Well,' I said, 'to the best of my powers. Shoes don't walk.'

Top Nun seemed to inhale her thin lips. She looked up and surveyed her constituency. We stood together while her eyes raked her charges, some four hundred girls running on the spot and blowing on their hands and chafing their blue thighs to stimulate blood flow, girls laughing and running in girl gangs and mocking and chanting, girls flashing at each other illicit pictures of pop stars, girls gossiping and flocking and crowing and ill-behaving; girls, not a few of them, stopped and transfixed and looking our way. Top Nun paused, considering. 'Do you know,' she said, 'I think that if you were to go and look again for your shoe bag, let's say, after school at four o'clock ... I believe you would find, Hilary, that it is exactly where it ought to be.'

What I felt, privately, was extreme anguish. I

thought that my parents could not afford to replace my shoes, or anything else that was lost; what was worse than this thought, was the thought of breaking it to my mother that in this place the girls also stole, that shoes walked, that books ripped themselves, that you were powerless against the wider society or against what ghosts did when your back was turned; that we had come to a new town, a new house, and that we were still not safe and unmolested. I didn't want her to know that *this* place was like *that* place; she was hoping so desperately that all places were not the same, she had staked her name on it, she had picked us up and run with us to a place that now looked no safer than the one where we'd been before. Thank you Sister, I said politely. I'll have a look. Well, you know, she said. If all is not well, Hilary. Her glance flickered again over her charges, now moaning in a slashing icy drizzle, pulling their sweaters over their heads and scurrying into lines to be let into afternoon school. If all is not well, I shall be very surprised. She spoke with an accent like the Queen's, but her upper lip was long, in the Irish style. She turned it up – blue as it was – into a tiny sadistic smirk.

It was well; of course it was. My shoe bag, by school-out time, was hanging on my allotted peg. My books were never torn again. It took me years to understand how the trick had been worked; that bold girls out to terrorise were so afraid of a sarcastic little

sister that they were reduced to infantile compliance
at the thought that she might be looking their way.
I was learning, always learning: power is negotiated,
acquired, given away, in more subtle ways than I had
understood when gun law and the power of the sword
were all that prevailed in my world. We must break
down the barriers of deference, as Tom Paine tells
us; this can be done quite politely, so that people
don't see that you are dismantling the things and
discreetly sneaking them away. My convent years
left me a legacy: a nervous politeness, an appearance
of feminine timidity which will probably stand me in
good stead if I am ever on trial for murder.

As for Top Nun: I learned her ways, she mine.
When I was in my last year at the convent, pupils
and staff voted me in, democratic, no deals, no bribes:
Top Girl. I was entitled to a gown of scarlet with a
gold stripe, which I wore with an air of sarcasm. Every
morning – this was the ritual of the Convent of the
Nativity – I stood on the stage of our vast assembly
hall – so big that it was hired out to Protestants
for the Mayor's Ball and vast civic junkets – and
at nine o'clock, as Top Nun took the stage, I would
say, on behalf of us all, 'Good morning, Sister Mary
Francis.'

Sometimes I was tremulous, because of things that
were happening at home. Sometimes I was breathless,
from belting in at the last minute, plunging my arms

into the gown held by an underling and vaulting on to the stage. Sometimes my tone was warm: if I'd had a good weekend. My hymn book sometimes had love letters tucked inside it: from Catholic boys, of course. I always, whatever, tried to greet her as if I meant it.

And she, speaking to me as if I were plural, and gazing out over the school, gazing into space, would reply, 'Good morning, girls.' She spoke into empty air, neutral, faint: as if she were biting on some edgeless, metaphysical glass. She was beyond shame, beyond embarrassment. After Vatican II – the great church council during which the sainted John XXIII told nuns to get hip and raise their hemlines – the whole school saw her sparrow legs, encased in thick stockings but somehow naked to our gaze; we didn't even make jokes about it. The nuns, too, were told to get out and about, and so Top Nun tried to learn to drive. She should have crushed her instructors, her examiners, with force of will; we could not believe – word leaked out – that she had to take her test again and again. When finally she passed, I surprised her, after morning assembly, with a huge, rather vulgar bouquet. You girls should not have known, she hissed at me, before accepting the flowers with an injured, ungracious simper.

One day when I was seventeen, almost hatched, almost ready to fly, I was standing at dusk in one of our cloakrooms, brushing out my hair. We were off in fifteen minutes to an after-school function,

to be bussed to Manchester to some other school
– I can't remember which, and little it matters –
for some inter-school debating torment, tournament,
something of that sort. I was our chief combatant, and
because of this I had to show up in my uniform and all
my friends – oh, sob, sniff – had gone home to change
into their miniskirts and put on their eyeliner. I was
sorry for myself, and doing the one thing I could:
so narcissistic that I was almost melting in to the
mirror, I was brushing out my hair. I planned to
wear it loose; who would say I couldn't? I sighed at
myself: who is like me? Nobody has hair like this. Oh,
what they would give! Brush and brush. I prolonged
the strokes so that each segment was drawn out by
the brush to its fullest length, before I released it, and
let it fall to join the fading light. Then I saw behind
me, in the mirror, a black-and-white dwarf. It was
SMF, Sister Mary Francis, Top Nun, crouching like
a court freak in the top of the frame: as if Velazquez
had painted us. Her eyes locked into mine. 'Ready?'
she said, unpleasantly.

'I was just . . .' my voice faded. Her coldest curl of
the lip said, she knew what I was *just*. Just admiring
myself, just doing a fair old Magdalen impersona-
tion. I felt caught out, diminished, yet made real,
fleshy, sordid.

But Sister had a lot invested in the debating com-
petition. For the first time, our little school was on

the way to winning. You didn't pick your subject, or your side. On the night when Sister caught me, I was preparing to debate the proposition we had drawn out of a hat: 'Karl Marx has done more for humanity than Jesus Christ.' I walked it. The final, everyone felt, was a formality; the strongest opposing team had been trampled into the dust.

Back at school, where our bus set us down, my friends pulled me to the convent door. Emboldened by three vodka-and-limes, a comrade studded her finger on the bell. The door fell open, nuns fell out; some of them with young and eager faces. 'Did ye win?'

Oh yes, my friends said. Communists one, Christians nil. Sister Mary Francis whisked around a corner, like a nasty sprite, and put her hand on my sleeve, and looked up into my face; once again I heard that giggle, sweet and clear as a running stream.

Here are some things that Jack did not agree with: breakfast, sport and illness.

He himself went out of the house in the morning on just half a cup of tea, which, my mother said, he could barely stomach.

Weaker people – that is, me – were allowed tea and toast.

Sport was rubbish, except for professional wrestling, which he watched on TV. History was bunk.

Illness was bunk. In the entire course of his school career, he had been 'never absent, never late'. Mr Neverill had become stepfather to Miss Neverwell, which was unfortunate for both of them.

A big question of Jack's was this: why are women always smiling? Look at them, he would say, pointing to the television screen. Smile, smile, smile.

Jack banned Shakespeare and mashed potato. Shakespeare was a subject, not a person. It was an unfortunate prescription of weak-minded women schoolteachers. It was an exam subject and could be tolerated if kept between the covers of my *Complete Works*, but it was not permitted to leak out into the real world – it should not be viewed on television, and especially not when it clashed with the wrestling. Shakespeare, when it occurred, was on the BBC. Wrestling was not. The BBC was bunk.

Potatoes should be chips or plain boiled in big chunks. It was forbidden to squash your potato surreptitiously with the side of your fork.

I was in trouble for sitting too close to the fire, 'pretending to be cold'. I was in trouble for being a girl, for being thirteen, for being fourteen. All my behaviour seemed to anger him, just by the fact of *being* behaviour: but silences, absences, were also a provocation to him. I have heard of fathers who said their daughters would grow up to be whores, or hairdressers. Jack said that I would grow up to

be a lab assistant. This would be my fate if my maths
didn't improve. Since Mrs Stevens and her Problems,
I had never been on terms with figures, but I had tried
to alter this when I was ten, spending hour after hour
working out huge multiplication and division sums
set by me for me. But when Jack took an interest in
my workings, I was swept by waves of hot panic. In
my first year at high school, he would spend an hour
sweating and wrestling over a few equations, trying to
insense me with their meaning, and my apprehension
rose as I saw it was half past eight already and I had
four other subjects to tackle that night before I could
go to bed.

It didn't seem to occur to Jack that I might have
a career outside the sciences; perhaps he didn't think
there was one. There were only little jobs that women
did: smile, smile, smile.

Life was a hair shirt to Jack. Like her, my mother
claimed, he had been forced against his natural grain,
forced too early out of education and into a job, into
earning money for his deserted mother and his sister.
Given his choice, she said, he would rather have been
an artist.

Unlike the doctor, Jack didn't name me. He called
me *they*. 'They always do this,' or 'they always that,'
he would sneer. I felt as if I were a survival, a relic,
a small squat subject race, whose aboriginal culture
was derided; like the Welsh, for example, a nation for

whom Jack had no time at all. Suppose you had grown up speaking Welsh, but now its use was prohibited. Even if you were obedient, if you were too scared to break the law, you would go on having Welsh thoughts, and the powers that be would always be scrutinising you, for evidence of subversion on your face. When you were silent, they'd be looking for clicks of your tongue and contractions of your jaw, to see if you were dissenting. They'd be listening at doors, to see if you talked in your sleep.

Jack liked the people around him to be in the same frame of mind as he was. So if he was tense, injured and gloomy, you would be in trouble if you went calmly about your business. If he was in the mood to be jocular, the whole household must sit before the TV set and roar at some low comedian. I kept out of the TV circle, and stayed in the dining room with my homework. He said, 'They never laugh.'

I would shut myself away and write history essays, derivative in content but of formidable length and grubby appearance. The pen called Swann moved as if it were writing on water; you wrote and hardly felt the grain of the paper. But the use of Swann was many years behind me, and we were not big on office supplies when I grew up. When I was sixteen I wrote in leaking and blotchy biro, a hundred pages of black bad handwriting, the quarto sheets held together – for want of staples or paper clips – with embroidery silk that I picked up from my mother's offcuts: coral, fern-green, the scarlet shade of the tip of butterflies' wings. The silk looked grimy after I'd twisted it up with my inky fingers, after I'd carried the pages about for a few days, scuffling footnotes into place and scratching second thoughts in the margin. Truth isn't pretty, I thought, and the pursuit of it doesn't make pretty people. Truth isn't elegant; that's just mathematicians' sentimentality. Truth is squalid and full of blots, and you can only find it in the accumulation of dusty and broken facts, in the cellars and sewers of the human mind. History's what people are trying to hide from you, not what they're trying to show you. You search for it in the same way you sift through a landfill: for evidence of what people want to bury.

There was tension in the air of our house, like the unbreathing stillness between the lightning and the thunder. In this space I went to and fro, clutching my essays with their slipping knots and scattering pages. Thin and pale, with long legs and a long fall of colourless hair, I was impeccably suited to my era, the sixties, though they were late in coming to the north. The girls at school were always combing through their biology textbooks to find something wrong with me. I was hyperthyroid perhaps, or anaemic. Envy, was the name of *their* disease.

Those were years of financial struggle for my

family, and strange expedients to make money. Appear-
ances had to be kept up, and our history suppressed.
People now will ask, what's so wrong, what's so difficult about running away and changing your names?
But there were big problems in that era, especially if
you only ran away for about eight miles: even if it was
eight miles over the county boundary into Cheshire.
In provincial England at that time, if you didn't want
trouble you pretended to be like everyone else. If you
were living with someone you weren't married to –
even if, and especially if, you were still married to
someone else – you called yourself just a regular family
and hoped people bought into your fictions; but at any
time a person who knew better might come along, and
explode them.

My brothers remembered little or nothing of their
early lives. Jack brought them up and Jack was their
father. They were English, without religion, and without a Hadfield accent. I was enrolled at a convent
school, nominally a Catholic, outwardly conforming,
though all – even Top Nun – knew my views. After
my bad time in the secret garden, my *mauvais quart
d'heure*, I stopped believing in an omnipotent God; I
believed in him as a pretty conceit for a year into high
school, but I didn't credit him with much pull, and
after I was twelve I didn't believe in him at all. And
as my great-uncles and great-aunts died one by one,
I lost my consciousness of being Irish. The Hadfield

accent never completely shifted, but it was my long memory that was the problem. The past could not be knocked out of me. As the decade wore on and my family became established in its new life, I felt like a death's head at a feast. Henry, my father, might as well have been dead; except that the dead were more discussed. Perhaps my mannerisms recalled him, as an unwelcome ghost by the fire: the clerkly droop of the head, the habit of reading a book as if your eyes were hoovering the words from the page. He was never mentioned after we parted: except by me, to me. We never met again.

After my first week at the convent, I went home to my mother, worried. 'Big girls at school', I told her, 'ask me why I've changed my name.' (Eight miles: a county boundary: Catholic gossip permeates civic barriers, runs freely between parish and parish, an underground polluted stream.)

'Tell them', she said, 'that it's for *private* reasons.'

I tried out this turn of phrase: private reasons. 'Oh yes,' the big girls said. 'We understand that. But we want to know what they are.'

Once you have learned habits of secrecy, they aren't so easy to give up. That is why this chapter is shorter than it might be.

When I was growing up, my stepfather Jack lived

in an emotional labyrinth through which I could not begin to follow him. Jack was a person who was loyal to what he believed; in those years, his mind was never changed. Facts in which he had faith were invested with great emotional weight – facts indeed were judgements, and if you knew a contrary fact you had better keep very quiet about it, since mere possession of it was an offence. Even when he was wrong he was right; that was the arrangement. His status as father and wage earner gave him a moral rightness that was separate from accuracy or even likelihood. He was right because he was entitled to be right.

I learned from Marx how the brute facts of economic interaction underlie our notion of human nature. I wished Marx would come for his tea and bring Engels, and that they would sit and squash their potatoes and see how far they got.

When I was eighteen I left home to go to the London School of Economics. My course was law, and my burning desire for equity made me peculiarly unsuited to the subject.

PART FIVE

Show Your Workings

B y the time I was twenty I was living in a slum house in Sheffield. I had a husband and no money; those things I could explain. I had a pain which I could not explain; it seemed to wander about my body, nibbling here, stabbing there, flitting every time I tried to put my finger on it.

When I packed my bags for London, at eighteen years old, I went to live in a women's hall of residence in Bloomsbury. It was a haven of warmth, calm and order. My university course was engrossing, and it was taught by lawyers and academics of stature and reputation. I got involved in student politics, in meetings that dragged on towards midnight. I didn't think it was a waste of time; student politics at the LSE had at least some crossover with the real world. The school was mostly postgraduate, and cosmopolitan. Whatever foreign event made the news, there was someone who would tell you about it, explain the background from their own experience. The rattling, down-at-heel, overcrowded buildings pleased me better than any grassy quad or lancet window. And I was doing well; my tutors were beginning to talk to me about where my interests lay, about how I might like to specialise, in my third year. One of them invited me into his office, which was the size of a modest broom cupboard, and said, go in for constitutional law, constitutional and administrative, you'll study under Professor Griffith; that's my strong recommendation to you. How do we delimit authority, where do the powers of the state begin and end? My path seemed to have taken a new turn; it seemed I was a step or two from success. I hugged myself and thanked my tutor, but I walked away thinking, third year, third year, by then I won't be here.

There are times in life when the next, clear, logical step seems one you can't take at all. I found it difficult to see myself completing my course, and emerging as a grown-up London person on the verge of a career. I seemed to have less money than other people. I had the state grant and – in theory at least – the small yearly contribution that my parents should make. I schemed to do without that contribution, to spare them the expense, but my schemes didn't work. The hall fees took a huge slice out of my grant and left me with little room for incidentals, but they covered heat and light, breakfast and supper; in between came a pot of yoghurt. In my second year, I was aware, I would not be able to stay in hall and would have to find somewhere of my own to live. Any place I could afford would be well outside the city centre, so I would have to budget for fares, instead of walking everywhere as I did at present. In those days, students didn't generally get term-time jobs to supplement their grants; your course demanded your full-time commitment. Intermittently through my first year, I worried about this, and about something more serious and long-term. I wanted to be a barrister. How was I to do this? The facts of life pressed in on me. I was female, northern and poor. My family would not be able to help me through my post-degree studies, or my pupillage – that is to say, the barrister's apprenticeship. Women barristers were then in a small minority. A few brave women from unhelpful backgrounds had crashed the system. I had assumed I would be one of them. But now my resolve was undermined. I was acquainted with the facts of life, with some unpromising arithmetic. Also, I was in love.

I had known this a while before I came to London, but by the time the calamitous fact was admitted, between myself and the boy who was in it with me, we had already chosen our universities, and secured places at different ends of England. He had just turned eighteen, I was six months younger. We couldn't do anything about the parting that loomed ahead of us, but we had decided to be married, whenever it looked possible: sooner than that, if by any mischance

I became pregnant. When we had a daughter, my lover said, he would like to call her Catriona; would that be all right by me? I was very happy about it. We were both admirers of Robert Louis Stevenson. *Kidnapped* was really our favourite, but we couldn't call our daughter David, or name her after Alan Breck. She'd have to be named for the sequel.

Like all my contemporaries, in those first years when the contraceptive pill was widely available, I only half believed I could coerce my body and suspected that it might have some filthy tricks in store; the filthy tricks would be on the line of putting a baby in your arms before you were ready. I assumed I would be able to have Catriona at a time of my choosing. I didn't know she would always be a ghost of possibility, a paper baby, a person who slipped between the lines. It's a pity we didn't like *Travels With A Donkey*. There's a good name for a ghost: Modestine.

In our year apart my boyfriend and I wrote to each other every day. There was a hiatus when the postmen went on national strike; I don't think it was to protest at us personally, though some of the letters were very weighty. In later years, we carried the correspondence about with us, in a plastic bin bag, but when we first went to work abroad we threw it away. After all, we were planning never to be parted again.

Though I was happy in my London life, I looked forward with a sick intensity to his arrival for week-end visits. He had to be smuggled in, and kept like contraband in my room, my room-mate quartered elsewhere and a whole corridor of girls sworn to complicit secrecy; it was like Malory Towers, but with sex. When the girl along the corridor had a boyfriend stay with her, the fire alarm rang in the small hours, and I met her among the crowds on Malet Street, two hundred girls turned out in their night attire into the winter cold. Her face was white, her eyes were staring. 'Where is he?' I whispered, and she hissed, 'I put him in the wardrobe.'

The expense of travelling, the logistical manoeuvres required, the wear-and-tear on the nerves, meant that the visits had to be well spaced-out. And gradually, I realised that my world was changing. Light and colour were draining from the streets, and even spring didn't restore them. The grey ache of absence was too much to bear; why bear it, if it could be remedied? I thought it could. By early summer, when my surroundings had taken on the chewed, grainy monochrome of crumpled newsprint, I went to the university authorities to put my case. Did they think I could go up to Sheffield, and continue my course there? My boyfriend couldn't come to me, I explained, because he was studying geology, and geology isn't portable. He had already chosen his mapping area and walked it at weekends, and it was easier to move one law student with a suitcase than to relocate a massive chunk of carboniferous limestone from the Peak District, four square miles of rock swarming with corals, nautiloids and the ancestors of starfish.

Sheffield University's law faculty was housed, in 1971, in a former maternity home, with ramshackle partitions and makeshift corridors. The students seemed dull, hostile, and pitifully young; they were my own age, in fact, but I felt I had different experiences and was older. They were afraid of their teachers, and before tutorials they stood in rigid knots outside closed doors, waiting, tension building between them; those rooms, full of the awe and anticipation of women's pain, were now darkened by juvenile dread of donnish sarcasm. But 'donnish' is pitching it too high perhaps; one of my tutors was a bored local solicitor who made it plain that he didn't think women had any place in his classroom. They were just a waste of space; they'd only go and have babies, wouldn't they?

Some people have forgotten, or never known, why we needed the feminist movement so badly. This was why: so that some talentless prat in a nylon shirt couldn't patronise you, while around you the spotty boys smirked and giggled, trying to worm into his favour. The birth control revolution of the late sixties had passed our elders by – educators and employers both. It was assumed that marriage was the beginning of a woman's affective life, and the end of her mental life. It was assumed that she neither could nor would exercise choice over whether to breed; poor silly creature, no sooner would her degree certificate be in her hand before she'd cast all that book-learning to the winds, and start swelling and simpering and knitting bootees. When you went for a job interview, you would be asked, if you were not wearing a wedding ring, whether you were engaged; if you were engaged or married, you would be asked when you intended to 'start your family'. Whether you were celibate, or gay, or just a sensible pre-planner, you had to smile and jump through the flaming hoops held up for you by some grizzled ringmaster, shifty and semi-embarrassed as he asked a girl half his age to tell him about her sex life and account for her next ovulation.

My transfer to Sheffield University was not as smooth as I had hoped. On paper, my first and second year fitted together. In practice, they didn't. While the LSE was occupied in wrenching its first-year law studies into some sort of social context, Sheffield was sneaking in extra property law, under the guise of legal history. I found myself at sea, both baffled and bored. My fellow second-years mostly intended to be solicitors. They were going into daddy's practice, or into their uncle's. I got into trouble by claiming mischievously that jurisprudence was all an elaborate bluff and that legal language was cognate with magic. 'Sign your name here or make your mark: pronounce a formula: abracadabra, you are man and wife. I put on a wig, I indict a scroll: abracadabra, your marriage is dissolved.' If you are right, said my tutor heavily, I suppose we may as well all go home. He stood up and clasped his arms behind his back, and looked out of his window, melancholy, towards the distant hills.

All the same, Sheffield was a good place to be if you were a student. The townspeople talked to you at the bus stop and in the shops, and they didn't seem to have any money either, so you could buy cheap cuts of meat and bargain tins and sustaining fresh loaves hot from the oven. Do you realise, I would ask my boyfriend, that at your tender age of nineteen, you both run a car and keep a mistress? The car was the product of his summer working in a factory that made cardboard boxes; his hands sliced to pieces, but pound notes stacking up. The car's labouring engine often jibbed at Sheffield's steep hills, and gaping holes in its bodywork were patched with a substance called plastic padding, but it hauled us across the moors to see his family; we made the trip often, as his father was sick. I cooked for us every night at my lodgings, an attic room in the house of a kindly, absent-minded divorced woman who didn't mind that two of us were trooping up her stairs.

There were two electric rings in my room, one for carbohydrate of the day – pasta, rice, potatoes – one for our meat or fish. We were ingenious cooks, and sat smiling over our yellow Formica table, as our dinner bubbled and simmered; I would be shivering slightly, because the only means of ventilation was an open window that admitted the piercing wind. One day, as I was hauling a great bag of potatoes uphill, my landlady stopped me at the gate. Her brow was furrowed. 'Ilary,' she said, 'why are you doing this?' I dumped my bag at my feet, and smiled up at her, bent double, massaging my carrying arm. 'You should be *going out*,' she said.

I flew out of myself, saw myself through her eyes: a small pale child with cropped hair, wearing a coat outgrown by one of her younger brothers. 'It's all right,' I said. 'Don't worry, I'm fine.'

I never quite understood what this was, this 'going out'. What was the gratification in it? It seemed to me, generally, just a polite prelude to sex; if you've got beyond politeness, why get dressed up and go off into the cold? You have a person you want to be with, whom you'd rather be with than be on your own; isn't that, by itself, a sort of fiesta? As for the grocery shopping: I liked to be able to say we ate well, that we stretched our small amount of money as far as

a proper meal every night. There was nothing left
over. And besides, I was trying to feed us up, trying
to pad us against the disaster to come. That was a dark
winter; the miners were on strike, and there were long
cold hours without electricity. On a January night, we
were called home, and the expected death occurred.

My boyfriend's father was called Henry. He was
fifty-three, a professional man, wry and studious, a
father of five. In summer he was a well man and in
September he was sick and the following January he
was dead: cancer. A year later, to the day, my grandfather would die of the same disease; more winter
journeys, over the dark Pennines, to stand about in
hospital wards while screens were drawn around beds.
But we were married by then, and living in a rented
room over a garage, a jerry-built extension which had
a leaking roof; and when we returned from the funeral,
we found that the cracks in the wall had grown wide,
and that an aggressive black mould had grown on our
food and on our clothes.

Married, why? Because in times of disaster, it's
what you do. When families are destroyed suddenly,
you pick yourselves up and glue yourselves together
to form new units. More practically, and immediately,
we married so that we could spend the night together,
so that he did not have to roll out of bed and roll
home over the midnight cobblestones; even the kindly
divorcée, thinking of her two growing children and

their moral development, would not let me have a man in the house till dawn. We had tried to find a place together, in anticipation of our marriage, but the landlords demanded certificates from the university, endorsements and validation on oath to say that we had really truly booked the priest and the registrar. They wanted no fornication among their Formica, they were not about to yield one curling inch of their old linoleum to the mad young seeking to gratify themselves. In mouse-dropping hallways we pleaded our purity of intent. But the faces were stony with rectitude: no room at the inn.

Yet not everyone was hostile to romance. Some comfortable soul could always be found in those days, to recall, 'They say two can live as cheaply as one.' Can they? My family fell out with me, and didn't fill in the forms for my subsistence grant. So we were about to find out if the saying was true.

Seventy-eight Roebuck Road was a back-to-back house; that is to say, it was one room deep, with a cellar, a room, a room on top of that, and an attic. It had one cold water sink, a shared outside lavatory, and a single metered gas fire. Even the hardy cockroach gave it the go-by, but a darting population of creatures we used to call 'silverfish' lived in the old chimney breast; they were harmless, I said to my husband, we used to have them at Brosscroft, they're OK, not dirty. I counted Roebuck Road as one of the greatest pieces of luck ever to come my way. We had not been able to afford the room over the garage: still less, the extra we might have been charged for growing the black mould. One of my tutors – a woman – had told me about a cheaper prospect; her cleaning lady lived there, but was moving on to something better.

No. 78 was the cheapest house in the world. We had to go right across town every fortnight to pay the rent, but the car took us, and even we, having paid the rent, could afford to eat. My grandmother gave us a water boiler to hang over the sink. My new mother-in-law gave us a cooker and some furniture. We slept on a sofa that flattened in the middle and so made into a bed. We couldn't get the stately family wardrobe upstairs, so it stayed down, its fine mirror reflecting the flickering of the silverfish as they busied cheerfully about their lives. I made stews, pies, cherry cakes, chocolate cakes and chocolate cherry cakes. I answered, as law students do, my weekly 'problems,' in the set legal language, and each week turned out essays which were simply a more prolonged exercise in sifting and shuffling the same chary formulations. I complained that law was wrecking my English style, which had been sturdy by the time I was sixteen, a little oak tree: that it was teaching me to equivocate and hedge, to stick to the literal and to lower my intellectual sights.

Show Your Workings

I complained I had a pain in my legs, and I went to the doctor: and that was my big mistake.

Writing about your past is like blundering through your house with the lights fused, a hand flailing for points of reference. You locate the stolid wardrobe, and its door swings open at your touch, opening on the cavern of darkness within. Your hand touches glass, you think it is a mirror, but it is the window. There are obstacles to bump and trip you, but what is more disconcerting is a sudden empty space, where you can't find a handhold and you know that you are stranded in the dark. Each day I was taking, though I didn't know it, a small step towards the unlit terrain of sickness, a featureless landscape of humiliation and loss. At Roebuck Road, the stairhead was dark; and some previous occupant had pinned, on the blank wall you saw as you descended, a poster with an owl on it. It was a child's owl, a simple and almost a cartoon owl, not less baleful for that. I wanted to rip it down, but I couldn't reach it.

Letters from the Inland Revenue arrived, tax demands addressed to a 'Mr Judas Priest'. These made us laugh. I set out my aspirin, one two three four five six. I swallowed them. Once, in error, I picked up and almost swallowed a shirt button, lying on the table waiting for me to sew it on.

*   *   *

'Sick?' said the doctor, down at the Student Health Service. 'Throw up? I'm hardly surprised. You do know that taking six aspirin is no more effective than taking three?'

I didn't. As it was double any ordinary pain, I'd thought I could double the aspirin. We weren't very sophisticated in those days. I don't think we even had paracetamol. I had a big bottle of a hundred aspirin, and I used to take whatever number I thought would get me through the day.

'Well, Miss—' said the doctor. He glanced down at his file, and a little jolt shot through him, as if he were electrified. Mrs?' he said. '*Mrs?* You've got married? Pregnant, are you?'

I hope not, I thought. If so, I've overdone it with the aspirin. It'll have fins. Or feathers. Three extra aspirin, three extra heads. I'll exhibit it. It will keep us in luxury.

'I'm on the Pill,' I said. An urge rose in me, to say, we are sexually very keen so I take three pills a day, do you think that's enough? But then a stronger urge rose in me, to be sick on his shoes.

I can see him, now that the years have flown; his crinkly fairish hair sheared short, his rimless glasses, his highly polished brogues. He was a nervous man, and when I bowed my head towards his feet he shifted them under his desk. I wasn't sick, not there and then. I put my hand across my mouth, and went outside, and threw up in the Student Health Service lavatories. It was quite a luxurious vomit, private and well-lit. At Roebuck Road, our facility was shared with next door, and you had to plough down their garden to get to it, so that at night dogs barked and householders with their torches came out shouting 'What's all this?' and you were caught in the cross beams, your loo roll in your hand.

I went home. 'What did the doctor say?' my husband asked.

'He said, don't take so many aspirin. I said my legs ached and he said it was accounted for by no known disease. Except one called idiopathic something-something.'

I didn't say how I had grinned, when he said 'idiopathic.' I knew it meant, disease about which we doctors have no bloody idea. So he had bridled, and swallowed the rest of the medical term; he wasn't, anyway, entertaining it as a possibility, he was just boasting, showing he remembered his textbooks. And my smile called his bluff; I shouldn't have smiled it. He was not on my side now. I thought that probably he never had been.

Go back, said my mister, grimly. You haven't really told him. How tired you are. And how upset.

I was upset, it was true. I couldn't bear my smashed

relationship with my family. That my brothers should think badly of me. That I should have no money to buy a present for Father's Day, only a bag of toffee, and nothing to give for Christmas but a box of biscuits and a bottle of wine.

That I had money to give even these was because of the intervention of a bureaucrat at County Hall in Chester, where lived the authority who paid (or not) my maintenance grant. For my visit I composed myself into pliant, pleading mode. We went to Chester by way of the grumbling, grunting, plastic-padded car. I went to see him in his office, the necessary man, the bureaucrat who was on my case. I explained that my father hadn't signed my forms to testify to his income. So therefore, he said, I could get no grant, not even the fifty pounds that every student got, even the rich ones: for those were the rules. I know this, I said, but you see I shall just have to sit here till the rules are amended in my favour, because if I don't get some money from you I'm out of house and home.

I don't remember his face, only his office, his desk, his chair, the slant of the light. He left the room. I studied his carpet, on which I had sworn I would be sleeping: unless I slept on his desk. It was a warm, blossoming, summer day: perhaps I could sleep in a flower bed? Sunlight rippled on magnolia walls. He came back smiling. I have got you fifty, he said, and let's see, hereafter, maybe it can be worked – there are always some strange circumstances . . .

Perhaps he was an angel. Perhaps a mortal, but one of the elect. I'm praying for him still, in a wild agnostic fashion. Hoping he wins the national lottery: I pray some irregular prayer like that. Or that he'd come to see me and I could make him a pie or a cake.

Go back, said my husband; tell them how you really are. Here you go, said the doctor, scribbling me a prescription; I think what you need is some anti-depressants. I was depressed, so I knew it made a kind of sense. Twenty-four hours later, I found I couldn't read; print blurred before my eyes. I went to the university library and tried to look up the side effects of the drug, but I was labouring under the obvious handicap. In those days, pills didn't come with a patient information leaflet. Your doctor had all the information you needed, and whether you could get it depended on whether you had pull, face and cunning. I had none of these.

I went to see my tutor in Equity, and said, look, Mr Loath (it wasn't his name, I didn't say it, it was just what the frightened spotty boys called him) look, Loath, I'm coming to your next session, but don't harass me, right? (Really, of course, I spoke to him much more nicely than this.) Loath, please understand that I've been prescribed some necessary drugs that mean I can't read my books. Blurred vision. Side effects, I said. Under my breath: you must have heard of side-effects? Loath gave me a puzzled look, as if he'd never heard of any such thing.

I tried some other tutors. I was asking for a week's grace, or perhaps a fortnight's, to audit my courses but not take part. Their reaction was all the same: why was I telling them this? The medical textbook (if I'd read it right, squinting, aslant) suggested that the blurred vision would last only a week or two, whereas the course of drugs lasted six weeks. Six weeks, in clinical practice, was the term set to depression; six weeks was a cure. After that, I was sure, I'd be happy. Never mind who was dead and how. Never mind how few the coins in my purse. I'd be up with the lark and rejoicing with the wrens: I'd be skipping up the hills of Sheffield, my pains vanished, my joints springing, swinging my bags of potatoes and self-raising flour as if they were feathers, as if I were self-raised myself; and scattering my careless laughter to the winds. For the time being, though, my spirits had sunk. The drugs seemed to be having an effect, but not the one required. The pangs of bereavement, of estrangement, had given way to a dull apathy. My sleep was broken and the climate of my dreams was autumnal, like the dim leaf-mould interior of a copse; their content was exhausting and yet somehow banal.

A day or two later, Mr Loath presided over his tutorial: the pasty, sweating, spotty boys, one other girl, and me. A small question of criminality was raised, and Mr L got testy: come along, come along, he said, do you know the maximum penalty under the Theft Act, do *you*, boy, or next boy, do *you*? I had to speak up and spare the boys, from their humiliation; oh, Mr Loath, I said, is it not ten years? Mr Loath, fuming with frustration, was just about to snap the arm of his spectacles; his fingers relaxed, and 'Thank goodness!' he said. And just as he replaced his glasses on his head, a pain sliced through me, diagonal, from my right ribs to my left loin. It was a new pain: but not new for long. It stole my life: it stole it for ten years and for a double term, and then for ten years more.

A short time later I was vomiting a good deal. I had finished the course of anti-depressants, but felt no more cheerful, and my GP did what you do when someone says she is vomiting: send her to a psychiatrist. I should like to say I protested, but I was willing enough. I thought perhaps I was a fascinating case. I had been tested for anaemia, but I wasn't iron-deficient. No one seemed to be able to think of another disorder to test me for, and if my body was not the problem it must be my mind that was acting up; I could believe this, and wanted my mind fixed. 'Psychosomatic' was the buzzword. Properly understood, the term suggests a subtle interaction between mind and body, between the brain and the endocrine system. Improperly understood, it means, 'it's all in the mind' – that is to say, your symptoms are invented. You've nothing better to do with your time. You're seeking attention.

Dr G, the psychiatrist, was remote and bald. He had as much chance of understanding a girl like me as he had of rising from his desk and skimming from the window on silver pinions. He soon diagnosed my problem: stress, caused by overambition. This was a female complaint, one which people believed in, in those years, just as the Greeks believed that women were made ill by their wombs cutting loose and wandering about their bodies. I had told Dr G, in response to his questions about my family, that my mother was a fashion buyer in a large department store; it was true, for at the end of the sixties she had reinvented herself as a blonde, bought herself some new clothes and taken up a career. Oh really, said Dr G: how interesting. Thereafter, he referred to her place of work as 'the dress shop'. If I were honest with myself, he asked, wouldn't I rather have a job in my mother's dress shop than study law? Wouldn't the dress shop, when all's said and done, be more in my line?

I saw Dr G once a week. He must have obtained

reports about me from my tutors, for he said, conscientious, hm, it says you're *very* conscientious.

Was I? I only turned in the work asked for. Didn't other people bother?

'And a *mind for detail*,' Dr G said, 'you have that.' I tried to imagine the other kind of law student, the kind who favoured the broad-brush approach, who took on the law of trusts, for example, with a grand generalist's sweep and dash. 'Tell me,' said Dr G, 'if you were a doctor, what kind would you be?'

I said politely that to be a psychiatrist must be interesting. No, pick something else, he said, something less close to home. I'd often thought, I said, that GPs had a challenging job, the variety of people and problems, the need for quick thinking – but no, I could see by his face that wasn't the answer required. Dr G sat back in his chair. I see you as a medical researcher, he said, one of those quiet invaluable people in the back room, unseen, industrious, unsung – a mind for detail, you see. And wasn't it the same, he asked, with law? If I did go on with my studies, wouldn't the niche for me be in a solicitor's office, conveying clients' houses – wasn't it just what people needed, at such a stressful time in their lives, to have the services of someone *very conscientious*, like me?

I could see her: a clerk very conscientious and quiet and dull, who wore snuff-coloured garb and filed herself in a cabinet every night and whose narrow heart fluttered when anyone mentioned a flying freehold or an ancient right of way. But you're not *looking* at me, I thought. I was quite thin; nausea was wearing me away. I left G's consulting room and stood on the pavement to consider this new version of myself. I felt as if I had been dealt a dull blow, but I didn't know which part of me ached.

The next time I went to Dr G's office I sat and wept. It was as if a dam had burst. I must have worked through a box of tissues, and no doubt it was his upset-girl ration for the whole month. Dr G spoke gently to me; said gravely he had not known that things were so bad. I had better have some stronger pills. And maybe a spell in the university clinic? I trucked off there, with my textbooks. At least now my husband would be able to study in peace for his finals. I wasn't easy company; I was labouring under a violent sense of injustice that may have seemed unreasonable to the people around me; I was angry, tearful and despairing, and I still had pains in my legs.

I think, in retrospect, that it would have been better if I had denied that I had pains in my legs, if I had taken it all back, or brightly said that I was well now. But because I didn't, the whole business began to spiral out of control. I still believed that honesty was the best policy; but the brute fact was, I was an invalid now, and I wasn't entitled to a policy, not a policy of my own. I feared that if I didn't tell the strict truth, my integrity would be eroded; I would have nothing then, no place to stand. The more I said that I had a physical illness, the more they said I had a mental illness. The more I questioned the nature, the reality of the mental illness, the more I was found to be in denial, deluded. I was confused; when I spoke of my confusion, my speech turned into a symptom. No one ventured a diagnosis: not out loud. It was in the nature of educated young women, it was believed, to be hysterical, neurotic, difficult, and out of control, and the object was to get them back under control, not by helping them examine their lives, or fix their practical problems – in my case, silverfish, sulking family, poverty, cold – but by giving them drugs which would make them indifferent to their mental pain – and in my case, indifferent to physical pain too.

The first line of medication, in those days, were the group of drugs called tricyclic anti-depressants – which I had already sampled – and also what were then called 'minor tranquillisers'; the pills marketed as Valium were the most famous example of the type. Highly popular in those days among overworked GPs, the minor tranquillisers are central nervous system depressants. They impair mental alertness and physical co-ordination. They dull anxiety. They are habit-forming and addictive.

The anti-depressants didn't seem to be having

much effect on me – or not the wanted effects, anyway, only the effects of making me unable to grapple with the written word, of making print slide sideways and fall out of the book. It didn't seem as if I would be able to sit my finals, Dr G said, but never mind: in view of my good work record, the university would grant me an aegrotat degree. Did I understand *aegrotat*? It meant 'he is sick'.

I muttered 'he, not she?' It would have been much healthier for me if I had stopped muttering, and kept smiling.

Valium, however, did work; it worked to damage me. Some people, given tranquillisers of this type, experience what is called a 'paradoxical reaction'. Instead of being soothed, they are enraged. One day I sat by the hearth at Roebuck Road and imagined myself starting fires – not in my own chimney, but fires in the houses of strangers, fires in the streets. Somewhere along the line, I seemed to have been damaged; I imagined myself doing damage, in my turn. I knew these thoughts were not rational, but I was obliged to entertain them; day by day I smouldered in a sullen fury, and when I saw a carving knife I looked at it with a new interest. I agreed to the clinic because I thought that, if I were to act on my impulses, someone would see me and stop me – before, at least, it got to arson and stabbing, and the deaths of strangers who had never harmed me at all.

After a day or two in the clinic I felt a little calmer. No one saw me as a danger; the danger was all in my own head. At first I came and went; I would go back to Roebuck Road during the day and do the cleaning. One day I went down to town to buy myself a nightdress. But because my vision was blurred, I misread the label, and came back with a size 16 instead of a size 10. 'Look at this monster garment!' I cried gaily to the nurses; I was having one of my less murderous days, and trying to lighten the tone. 'Look what I bought!'

My nightdress, I found, was viewed in a grave light. Why had I bought it? It was a mistake, I said, you see I . . . Didn't you hold it up? they asked me. Well, no, I, I just liked the pattern, I . . . Didn't you remember what size you were? Did you feel you didn't know? Yes, I know my size, but you see, my eyesight, it's misty, it's because of the drugs I . . . oh, never mind.

But they wouldn't drop the topic. It was obviously characteristic of mad girls to buy big nightdresses. Every time I spoke I dug myself into a deeper hole.

Dr G came to see me. Well, and what was I doing with myself now that I was free from my struggles with my textbooks? I have written a story, I offered brightly. It was a long story – that is to say, a short story, but long as these things go. Short but long, said Dr G. Hm. And what was it about? A changeling, I said. A woman who believes her baby has been taken away, and a substitute provided in its place. I see, said Dr G, and where and when did this occur? In rural Wales, I said, funnily enough. (I'd never been to Wales.) I don't have to say the date, but it feels like the early 1920s. I mean, judging by their furniture and clothes. Does it? said Dr G. It's a time well before social insurance, anyway, I said. The doctor won't come up the mountain to see them because they can't pay. I see, said Dr G. And how does it end? Oh, badly.

If you didn't respond to the first wave of drugs – if they didn't fix you, or you wouldn't take them – the possibility arose that you were not simply neurotic, hypochondriacal and a bloody nuisance, but heading for a psychotic breakdown, for the badlands of schizophrenia, a career on a back ward. To head off this disaster, doctors would prescribe what were then called the major tranquillisers, a group of drugs intended to combat thought disorder and banish hallucinations and delusions.

The next time I saw Dr G he forbade me to write: or – more precisely – he said, 'I don't *want* you writing.' He put more energy into this statement than any I had heard him make. He seemed as remote as ever, and yet inexpressibly angry. 'Because –' he added; and broke off. He was not going to impart to me what came after 'because'.

I said to myself, if I think of another story I will write it. In fact, I didn't think of another story for quite some years – not a story of the long but short type – and when I did I sent it to *Punch* and what I got back was not a malediction but a cheque. The changeling too paid off, in time, in a novel published in 1985; the setting was not rural Wales, nor the 1920s, but the present day in a prosperous and dull Midlands town. The novel contained mad people, but no one suggested its author was mad. It's different, somehow, when you've received money for your efforts; once you've got an agent, and professionalised the whole thing.

The first drug I was given was called Fentazine. That would do the job, Dr G thought.

Do you know about akathisia? It is a condition that develops as a side-effect of anti-psychotic medication, and the cunning thing about it is that it looks, and it feels, exactly like madness. The patient paces. She is unable to stay still. She wears a look of agitation and terror. She wrings her hands; she says she is in hell.

And from the inside, how does it feel? Akathisia is the worst thing I have ever experienced, the worst single, defined episode of my entire life – if I discount my meeting in the secret garden. No physical pain has ever matched that morning's uprush of killing fear, the hammering heart. You are impelled to move, to pace in a small room. You force yourself down into a chair, only to jump out of it. You choke; pressure rises inside your skull. Your hands pull at your clothing and tear at your arms. Your breathing becomes ragged. Your voice is like a bird's cry and your hands flutter like wings. You want to hurl yourself against the windows and the walls. Every fibre of your being is possessed by panic. Every moment endures for an age and yet you are transfixed by the present moment, stabbed by it; there is no sense of time passing, therefore no prospect of deliverance. A desperate feeling of urgency – a need to act – but to do what, and how? – throbs through your whole body, like the pulses of an electric shock.

You run out into the corridor. A man is standing there, gazing dolefully towards you. It is your GP, the man at the Student Health Service, the man with the rimless glasses and the polished brogues. The tension rises in your throat. Speech is dragged and jerked out of you, your ribs heaving. You think you are screaming but you are only whispering. You whisper that you are dying, you are damned, you are already being dipped into hell and you can feel the flames on your face.

And the answer to this? Another anti-psychotic. An injection of Largactil knocked me into insensibility. I lay with my face in the pillow as the drug took effect, and sank into darkness; as I ceased to panic and fight, the hospital sheets dampened, and wrapped around me like ropes.

After I woke up, I was maintained on Largactil, to combat my madness. It was not a friendly drug; it made my throat jump and close, as if someone were hanging me. This is how a mad person appears to the world – lips trembling, speech fumbling and jerky. You can say, this is the drugs you know, this is not me; I am quite all right, inside myself. They say, yes dear, of course you are; have you taken your pill?

But then it was the end of term, the end of the year. My course of studies was over. The university's responsibility was ended. I was discharged from the clinic. I went home, and was sane. The drugs wore off; I no longer twitched and jumped. I could have passed for normal in any company. My legs didn't seem to ache so much; I had more abdominal pain, but I knew better than to mention it. For a time I claimed to be well.

But it was not so easy to shake off the events of the last year. The problem was the names of those drugs I had 'needed', spelled out like evil charms in my medical notes. Fentazine, Largactil, Stelazine. If I set foot in a GP's surgery – as I did, when I grew increasingly sick – I ran the risk of being prescribed a dose of them that would knock an elephant off its feet. Then there was my old friend Valium, which I knew I shouldn't go near: not unless I wanted to be arrested.

So when in time I went back to a doctor, I said I had backache, nausea, vomiting, that I was too tired to move. My GPs – to a man, and a woman – suggested a test to see if I was anaemic. I never was. They had no other suggestions; except perhaps some Valium: and a little spell away might do me good? By the time I was twenty-four I had learned the hard way that whatever my mental distress – and it does distress one, to be ignored, invalidated, and humiliated – I must never, ever go near a psychiatrist or take a psychotropic drug. My vision blurred, in those days, entirely without the help of the anti-depressants. Sometimes there were gaps in the world: I complained one day that the front door had been left open, but the truth was that I just couldn't see the door. Sometimes it seemed that some rustling, suspicious activity was going on, at the left side of my head, but I couldn't put a name to what it was. I couldn't put a name to lots of things, my speech came out muddled: I called a clock's hands its fingers, and a chair's arms its sleeves.

I was all right if I stuck with abstractions, ideas, images. And some days I was half well. I had a job, but I needed a pursuit, I thought. I went to the library and got out a lot of books about the French Revolution. I made some notes and some charts. I went to a bigger library and got more books and began to break down the events of 1789–94 so that I could put them into a card index. I was *very conscientious* and with *a mind for detail*. If you had been having a revolution you would certainly – at such a stressful time in your life – have needed the services of someone as conscientious as me. I began to read about the old regime, its casual cruelties, its heartless style. I thought, but I know this stuff. By nature, I knew about despotism: the unratified decisions, handed down from the top, arbitrarily enforced: the face of strength when it moves in on the weak.

One day, on an escalator in a department store, a man put a hand up my skirt. Enough, enough, I thought. I turned around and punched him in the eye. I got off at the top of the escalator and walked away.

I didn't like the world I was living in. It didn't seem too keen on me.

I was too sick to do a responsible job, a professional job. I got a job as a saleswoman, and I thumbed my nose at Dr G; I started to write a book. I wrote and wrote it. Time passed. I moved to another country, another continent. Still I wrote it and wrote it.

Christmas week 1979. I was twenty-seven years old. I was in St George's Hospital in London having my fertility confiscated and my insides rearranged. When I was admitted, I knew I was very ill, but I didn't know quite how bad things might be, and for a time there was no agreement on the nature of what ailed me. Only that it was physical; only that I had a pain and it was real: only that it was a disease Valium wouldn't cure.

My life had moved on by then, far from its early confines. We had wanted to travel, to see the world;

my husband had exchanged carboniferous limestone for the sands of the Kalahari, fossils for diamonds. For three years we had lived in a small town in Botswana, a railway line settlement, where geologists and agriculture specialists rumbled over the unmade roads in four-wheel drives, where ticks and mosquitoes bit, where the days were short and hot and monotonous, and I sat behind the insect mesh of my veranda frowning over my card index, documenting the fall of the French monarchy, the rise of the Committee of Public Safety. I had pressed the juice of meaning from every scrap of paper I had brought with me, every note on every source. The book was finished now. But so, it seemed, was I. When we came home to England on leave, my book went to a publisher who offered to look at it. I went to a consultant who offered to look at me.

In the beds around me were women with complications of pregnancy, who were trying to hang on to their babies; women having abortions; women having their fertility ended by choice. The latter group were two cheerful middle-aged Londoners, a little worn and raddled by life, who complained at the routine discomforts, the marching up and down corridors and waiting in a draught to have blood samples taken; even their complaints were cheerful, and they really amounted to grumbling about the fact that for a couple of days they weren't in charge, because they were used to a situation where what they say, goes. They had taken this decision, they, for themselves: another baby, no thank you! They called the surgery 'having my tubes tied'; I pictured the surgeon hauling ropes, shouting 'heave-ho!' and consulting a book of knots. On my right there was a silent Turkish girl in her early twenties, having a termination which she was not, I suppose, discussing with her family; she wanted a cigarette, she said, just a little draw would soothe her. After the operation she appeared to have greenish-dark bruises around her eyes, as if someone had undertaken to knock sense into her. The bruises deepened to caverns, then lightened to a jaundiced tan. Then she was gone, discharged. When she climbed out of bed you saw her vitality, her dark bandy legs, her strength. She would have, you thought, just as many children as she liked.

Her fellow abortionee was opposite me, a tow-headed sixteen-year-old on her second termination. We hopped from bed to bed, Kirsty and I, sitting each at the foot of the other. She told me about her life. She went out to dance and to shoplift a little and if anyone looked at the boy she happened to be with she would belt them around the head; isn't that right, she said, and we agreed that yes, it was the only thing to do. More perplexed than malicious, she called the nurses by whistling for them; she didn't understand their genteel nursey euphemisms, and when they handed her a flask and asked her to pass water she came across to ask if I knew what the fuck they were talking about.

Kirsty was taken to theatre to have her termination; believing that she had no chance of looking after her body, of regulating her future fertility, the surgeon fitted an IUD while she was under anaesthetic. But then the device fell out, one night when she was in the bathroom; she haemorrhaged, fainted with shock, and cracked her head open on the washbasin. Her life, you felt, would always be like this – the handing out of attrition, without regard to justice; fate would overreact to an ungoverned temper and the impulses of a generous heart. She had adopted me on my first day on the ward; I wasn't, she thought, getting my due. Until some time after I was admitted, the nurses could not manage to get a doctor up to the ward to organise pain relief for me. The strong pills I had brought with me were taken away, and I was given a Panadol, an over-the-counter remedy for everyday discomfort. A hot bath was promoted as the remedy for my pain; I laughed. That first night, I lay on the bed, my knees drawn up. Kirsty shouted at the nurses. 'Look at her, look at her,' she roared. 'Give her sumfin.' And they did – a rare opportunity – they told me it was my turn to push around the cocoa trolley. My turn, though I'd only just arrived! So I rolled off the bed and did it. 'Cocoa? Horlicks? Sugar with that?' I was not quite able to stand up straight: some inflamed growth inside me was bending me at the waist, pulling my abdomen, knotted with pain, down towards my knees. Silliness, I suspect, had set in; some endocrinological compassion-centre was flooding my brain with substances that suggested nothing now mattered very much.

I had been admitted without any certain diagnosis. The professor in charge of gynaecology had, in a civil way for which I remain grateful, found me a bed at short notice. Provided I didn't mind being in hospital for Christmas, he said, they could have me in about the 20th and operate before the feast. I had felt bleak, on the journey down the motorway – not afraid, but feeling in a childish way that there was nothing to look forward to. After two Christmases in Africa, when I'd missed my family badly, this was not what I had planned. When the professor had examined me at Outpatients, a week or two earlier, I'd bled everywhere, on to his latex hands and the sheet beneath me. I thought he'd have been hardened to that, but he said, 'I am afraid I am hurting you. I am sorry. I will stop now.' I would have liked it if curiosity would have propelled him onwards: pushing into the unseen, smoking meat of my body, and finding out its truth.

How can I write this, I wonder? I am a woman with a delicate mouth; I say nothing gross. I can write it, it seems; perhaps because I can pretend it is somebody else, bleeding on the table.

But at the time, I came to the vertical, sickly swaying. I mopped myself up and got into my clothes. I sat in a chair: black vinyl, splayed legs, the ridge of its back hard against my spine. You say you think it's endometriosis, he said. There's a good chance you're right. But he didn't look a happy man. Could it be anything else? I asked. How we conspire, not to speak the word 'cancer.' His eyes slid away. Oh well, he said, if not endometriosis, then pelvic inflammatory disease, it is a thing to consider. I said, no I don't think so really. He nodded. He didn't think so, either. He said by the way, is it, should I, am I speaking to Doctor McEwen? I looked up to see if he was being sarcastic. No, I said, I'm not a doctor, why would you think that? Only, he said, your terminology is precise. Ah well, I thought. If only you knew me: *conscientious*, with a *mind for detail.* Little Miss Neverwell had graduated at last.

Endometriosis is a gynaecological condition with a dazzling variety of systemic effects. It is not rare, though mercifully it is rare for the disease to run on, unrecognised, for as long as it did in me, and it is rare for it to do such damage. Because of the number of symptoms it throws up it is sometimes hard to diagnose. It is always hard to diagnose, for a doctor who doesn't listen and doesn't look. It is comparatively easy if you are the patient, and get into your hands a good textbook with a comprehensive account of its effects.

A few months earlier – in the remoteness of my small town on the fringes of the bush – I had thought, once again: enough's enough. My doctor (his dusty downtown surgery darkened by eucalyptus trees) seemed disinclined to investigate, though happy to prescribe me stronger and stronger pain relief. Whatever he gave me (and however much alcohol I knocked back to accompany it) the pain grew over the top. So one day I went up to the capital, to the university library, and combed through the medical books. I found a textbook of surgery, with a female figure, her organs clearly depicted, and black lines – like the long pins with which they used to stick witches – striking through her hips and ribcage, carrying a name for each organ. For each organ, there was a pain, and of each pain, I had a sample.

I learned next how the disease process worked. The endometrium is the lining of the womb. It is made of special cells which shed each month by bleeding. In endometriosis, these cells are found in other parts of the body. (How they get there is a matter of dispute.) Typically, they are found in the pelvis, in the bladder, the bowel. More rarely, they are found in the chest wall, the heart, the head. Wherever they are found, they obey their essential nature and bleed.

Scar tissue is formed, in the body's inner spaces and small cavities. It builds up. It presses on nerves and causes pain, sometimes at distant sites. The scar tissue forms an evil stitching which attaches one organ to another. Infertility is a distinct possibility, as the organs of the pelvis are ensnared and tugged out of shape. Endometriosis in the intestines make you vomit and gives you pains in the gut. Pressure in the pelvis makes your back ache, your legs ache. You are too tired to move. The pain, which in the early stages invades you when you menstruate, begins to take over your whole month. Lately I had known days of my life when everything hurt, everything from my collarbone down to my knees. But hey! There was nothing wrong with my ankles. My feet were performing nicely. And I could still think, and depress the typewriter keys. Stop complaining! I thought. Look where complaining gets you! In the madhouse.

Along with endometriosis goes, not infrequently, a hormonal disarrangement that shows itself as a severe premenstrual syndrome. In my case, it manifested in the prodromal aura of migraine headaches. Migraine, I had to learn, was not just a sick headache. It was a series of linked neurological phenomena of remarkable diversity. It was within the migraine aura that my words came out wrong, that the door disappeared into a black space: it was within the aura that I heard the dull hum and the muttering on the left-hand side of my head. Migraine stirred the air in dull shifts and eddies, charged it with invisible presences and the echoes of strangers' voices; it gave me morbid visions, like visitations, premonitions of dissolution. For a time, when I was eight years old, my field of vision was filled with a constant, moving backdrop of tiny skulls. As a student, I had told Dr G about them, in a burst of frightened confidence. 'Black on a white ground, skulls skulls skulls, the size of my little fingernail, unrolling,' I said. 'Unrolling, like a satanist's wallpaper.'

Dr G smiled a wintry smile. 'Ah well,' he said. At this stage, I was only a neurotic, not the full-fledged madwoman I would become when he upped my dosage. 'Ah well.' His voice was soothing. 'We all have our little metaphysical fancies.'

1979: I must admit that the very act of climbing into the hospital bed had brought me a kind of relief. I could stop pretending to be well. The odd thing, though, as I had already observed, was that the staff were inclined to treat the patients as malingerers. We could see them huddled at their nurses' station, flicking through our notes and discussing our body parts. Young girls with flaky cervixes were probably no better than they should be, and anything in the pelvic inflammatory line attested to a vibrant sex life. Pregnant women weren't sick, women wanting abortions weren't sick, and as for the sterilisation brigade, they should probably be up and scrubbing the latrines. (That wouldn't have come amiss.) And as for me – I soon got a jolly diagnosis. The Senior Registrar examined me and thought I was pregnant. He winked at me. That's a baby in there, he said, confidently patting my swollen abdomen. He ran off to get a foetal heart monitor.

But there was no baby. Not Catriona, not Modestine: not anyone, only the ghost of my own heartbeat, amplified to the outside world. Oh well, the registrar said. Looks like I was wrong, eh?

The houseman came, to take a history. He was very new and young, with a starter moustache, which could be studied bristle by bristle; some bristles stuck out at a right angle to his skin. I kept my eye on it, and the movements of his mouth. You are very young, he said, and I am going to ask the professor, yes yes (he got up his resolve) I am going to talk to the professor, I am going to ask him if he can make a neat low incision, so that afterwards, you will be able to wear a bikini. He looked almost tearful. I nodded. I knew he would not be able to effect this, but I liked it that he cared so much. It is strange, to expose your soft girlish body to a man of your own age, who has not yet acquired dispassion but wears a white coat. In fact, I said, I never wear a bikini because I am too – I wanted to say, modest. But what modesty was left? I'd had more gynaecologists than I'd had lovers; alien fists in my guts. I said, you see, I am too white for a bikini. Too pale. I burn. Of course, he said. But all the same. He got up, flustered, his clipboard almost spilling his notes. At the bed's end, he turned and smiled, and winked at me.

Two days after I was admitted I needed to have an ultrasonic scan. For this I needed to cross London. St George's Hospital at Hyde Park Corner was in its last weeks of occupation; it was gaunt, grubby and nearly empty. My ward was almost the last to be kept open, I was told, and for the hi-tech stuff I needed to go to the new St George's at Tooting. I expected them to bring my clothes up the ward, but I was told, no, you have to go in your dressing gown, that's how patients go.

The only such garment I owned, myself, was a black satin wrap with a plunging neckline. But before I had been admitted to hospital my kind, practical cousin Beryl had said that she didn't think it would do, and lent me a green velour item, cosy and modest, that came to my ankles and buttoned up to the neck. I was very glad of it, when told I was to go by taxi to Tooting. They would organise the taxi, they said, no worries. Oh, I said to myself, I don't have to go out on the street and whistle for it? And, they said, they'd send someone to escort me.

Before I began the journey, I was to drink as much water as I could possibly bear to drink, to distend my bladder, which was a good thing for a reason nobody explained. In a way, you didn't want to ask. What if they didn't know? There was a trade-off in ignorance going on. They told me nothing, and I didn't ask questions in case I was shocked by finding how much they didn't know. I waited, sitting on my bed, pensively swigging from a hospital tumbler.

'Here's Della!' somebody shouted.

'Hello, hello!' Della shouted back. She rolled in like an Oscar candidate, like the belle of the ball. 'Wha-ay, Della!' rose the shout. Della whooped back. I know a character when I see one. And oh God, how a character shrinks my flesh with dread. I took one final sip of water.

Della was a Jamaican auxiliary, in her fifties or sixties. She was very wide, so that you felt you couldn't quite see around her. People must feel that about me, nowadays, but I don't think I block the light like Della did. She had a broad forehead and she glowered. She reminded me of a bison; not a bad thing, really, because as a child I liked the bisons at the zoo; they would stand near the fence, breathing bulkily, while you wormed your finger through the netting and scratched the expanse of sparse hair between their ears. But depend upon it: once on the open range, they could charge you down.

It was Della who was my promised escort to Tooting. They brought a wheelchair up to the ward. 'To take you to the taxi,' they said. But I said (maybe I just thought) I can walk, you know that, you make me walk, last night you invited me to operate the cocoa trolley . . . But they were insistent. They said it was a rule.

I was wheeled to the entrance and packed into a taxi with my bison. 'Wotcha, Della!' said the porters at the main door (or some other vile mock-cockney exclamation). Della had, I suppose, been given a letter to hand to someone at the other end, but she didn't seem to know why we were going to Tooting together, regarding it with levity and as a kind of holiday treat. She hollered back to the porters, 'Ray, what! Gwine Tootin, see yer, wot?'

The door slammed. We inched forward into the traffic of Hyde Park Corner. The driver kept his glass screen closed. But chat ran out of Della, chat chat chat. Who was I and why there, for what? I replied, a steady even flow of answers, censored against self-pity, censored against the personal, my face turning again and again to the taxi window. It took a long time, that journey, through the midday traffic, inching south, crossing the Thames. I have never come to terms with London as a city, but I like to look at it silently, from taxi windows, and appreciate it for what it is, and for how it makes me feel provincial.

On this day I felt possessed by the idea that I might not see it again. Even two days in the enclosure of a hospital ward changes your vision, and the buildings to me seemed distant and heroic, like the buildings of a dream city. I felt emotional, but couldn't put a name to my emotion. My bladder, which had been attacked by the disease process, had swollen obediently, and already I had a pain: a new sort of pain, quite a change really. Della was talking, loosely, fluently. I was replying to everything she said. Then she began a new story. My mind rejoined her. She told me about her youngest daughter, only eighteen, who had gone into hospital five years ago to have an operation on her hand. 'Just a little swellin,' Della insisted. 'I told her, don't you bother about that. Would she listen? Would she listen? Ho no!'

I swivelled from the window. For much of the journey till now I hadn't known what Della was talking about, but surely this was something I could understand? And how did it go for your daughter, I asked, did it work out all right, did they fix her up? Ho no! Della said. It all went wrong when they put her under. She's, like, a vegetable now. She got her brain destroyed. Vegetable's what they call it.

She spoke dispassionately, as if she were talking about a Martian. The law student in me was sick, but not entirely dead. In almost any circumstance, I would have leaned forward – *conscientious, mind for detail* – and said, you had a claim for negligence, did you get a good solicitor? I would have been slow to censure Della, for bringing up such a gloomy precedent, and considered that in fact she might have done me a favour: it gave me something other than my pains to think about. Did the hospital admit liability, and what damages did you get? Five years, I thought – five years, the case could still be enmeshed in the system. Only part of my mind flinched from what she had told me. The other part was about to ask her for the figures, for the dates. I was about to speak.

But then Della did a terrible thing. She let her head sag forward and her jowls hang, and she imitated her daughter's speech. 'She goes, Ma, Ma Ma. La, la, la. That's all she can do.' Della protruded her tongue. She grunted. 'Ma, ma, ma. La, la, la.' She lolled her head on her thick neck. 'Ma, ma, la, la.' At length, after time for consideration, Della put her tongue back in.

We travelled the rest of the journey in silence. The taxi driver put us down at the wrong entrance. Della seemed to know where we ought to be, and we set off together, she with unclouded brow, as if rolling across the grassy plains, me in my dressing gown and bare feet in slippers: bending a little over my pain, as if I were brooding. I had come from the heat of Africa, at the hottest time of year, and we were in December. In fairness, I must say, it was neither raining nor snowing. It was one of those days so near the end of the year that it won't put the effort in: only a stray sullen flake drifted down, out of a sullen sky.

I had worked in a hospital, at one stage in my career, and understood medical signposts, so I wasn't happy with Della's choice of destination. But she insisted. She kept charging, her bison head down; I had to follow her. I wanted to crouch down, on the gravel path, and urinate beneath my skirts, like Marie Antoinette on the way to execution; it is a sad detail of that sad life, which in my manuscript about the Revolution I had thought long and hard about suppressing, but had not. Della led me to the liver unit, where people thirty years my senior were standing in line. They were waiting for scans, it was true, but special ones, peculiar to them. They were yellow, bloated people, who resembled each other, who seemed to have joined the same family. None of them spoke to me. They just looked. They were stooped, like me. They held their abdomens draped over their forearms, holding up their own swags of flesh: like debutantes scooping up their trains to nip out of Buckingham Palace after their presentation.

A nurse shook his head at Della. He pointed. We backed off, away from the yellow people. I looked into the moons of their faces and they looked back at me, tolerant, indifferent perhaps. We set off again, me and Della, out of the liver unit and into the open air, up the gravel walks and down. The cold was raw and wet, like a salt bath. When I got to the right place, they were expecting me. Perhaps they had been expecting me for the last hour, but they didn't criticise. A technician, kindly but dispassionate, slicked jelly on to my abdomen. It reminded me of Swarfega, a product with which the men in my life degreased their hands after tampering with a car engine. Perhaps the hospital could fix me, with some plastic padding? The technician loomed above me and rolled me with a roller. Lifting my head, I saw the pictures on the screen. It didn't look sensible, it didn't look reasonable, and perhaps he didn't think so either. But he was helpful in pointing out the salient features. 'Nice full bladder,' he said, 'I expect you can't wait to get rid of that.' He showed me the blossoming growths around my ovaries. For the first and last time, I saw my womb, with two black strokes, like skilled calligraphy, marking it out: a neat diacritical mark in a language I would never learn to speak.

After the rolling was over, I was allowed to fall from the examination table, and urinate. When we got back to St George's, after another hour in a taxi, Della lolloped out of the cab and I followed gingerly, setting my slippered feet on the pavement. The porters shouted 'Whoa, Della! Wha-ay, ducks!'

'Bin Tootin,' she bawled.

'That's our gel,' the porters bawled back. They ran out a wheelchair and looked at me expectantly. I'm not getting in that, I said, don't be ridiculous; I've run halfway round south London in my dressing gown.

But you have to, they said, aghast. There's no two ways about it. We can't have you walking; what a notion! It's more than our job's worth.

Della was singing now, her attention elsewhere. Oh, if it's your jobs, I said. I wouldn't like to get you sacked. That's the way! they said. I sank into the wheelchair for the ride up to the ward.

As Christmas approached, the ward emptied. The cheerful women went home, sterilised, healed, still grumbling. A husband brought a suitcase for a young wife who had been caught in the early stages of cervical cancer – cured, she thought, she hoped. In bed she had looked like a ten-year-old boy, buttoned up inside a sensible warm top, her blonde hair tousled, her sharp face peaky. Now when the bed curtain swept back she stood straight and slim in three-inch heels, her angles encased in careful, beautiful clothes, which fitted her so exactly that you knew they had been made, by or for her; the precise hemline, the loose wool coat with its calibrated swing. She shook her head, and her thick blonde bob, precision-cut, settled into place, grazing her shoulder pads; she picked up her burnished leather bag, and stepped out into the rest of her life.

London emptied. The traffic stilled at Hyde Park Corner. A young woman remained in an opposite bed, six months pregnant, her face mottled with fever; she had a kidney infection and was, in the ward's parlance, 'poorly'. When the antibiotics began to work she sat up and looked about her with misty, Celtic eyes; her dark hair filmed the white pillow.

When the kidney girl sat up, it was already the eve of my surgery. No one had agreed yet on the nature of my problem. My husband had been told that, in the event that the growths were malignant, he should expect my death. I had not been given the message, but I didn't really need it. I stubbornly believed in my own diagnosis. If I was right, I would survive.

Many hours after dark, the carol singers came. I was in the bathroom at the time, standing with my back to the dark mirror. I had begun to feel, not afraid but very lonely; I had given way to self-pity, and tears were springing out of my eyes when they piped up with 'Once in Royal David's City'. I stood till it was over, leaning against the wall. Then I heard a woman say, in a sweet bossy voice, 'Perhaps you would care to choose a carol, dear?' And Kirsty laughed: a long peal, like glad tidings. They had swooped on Kirsty because she was in the first bed they came to; they had handed her a hymn book, and when I shot out of the bathroom she was holding it as if it were hot, and her laughter was the sound of her incredulity. I took the book from her; she darted a grateful glance. I flicked the pages over, and asked for 'God rest you merry, gentlemen'. The singers complied, though they looked a bit disappointed at such an old-fashioned choice. But I was thinking of our surgeons, coming tomorrow to cut me up; it was the last thing they would do, before going home to their families to carve the Christmas fowl.

After the singers had gone Kirsty fell into a dead sleep. I sat on the end of the kidney girl's bed and we smoked a cigarette. 'Ladies, back to bed!' the staff cried. I was the only one up, but they made me plural because they didn't care to confront me. Eventually I kissed the kidney girl goodnight, stroking back her dark hair; there was no one else to do it. I shuffled across to my own bed and edged myself beneath the covers. The mound of my abdomen was almost as big as kidney girl's pregnancy, and they still hadn't sorted out pain relief. They gave me a sleeping pill, but it would have taken a mallet to knock me out. I was not afraid, but my brain was active.

In the silence of the night, towards two o'clock, came an African woman in trouble, rocking her head from side to side, on a stretcher which had taken on the aspect of a bier. Two men, their faces stricken, walked behind her. The cold had given them an ashy hue, and they carried woollen hats, which they wrung between their hands.

I was brought up as a Christian, insofar as a Catholic may be so called. (My grandmother thought you didn't want to be reading the Bible, she thought it was a Protestant book.) Christians are given, for their psychic support, the model of a man dying in extreme agony. As Catholics we were encouraged in my childhood to follow the 'Stations of the Cross', praying certain prayers at each depiction of the stages of Christ's Passion. We were taught to be thankful that, whatever was in store for us, it wasn't crucifixion: unless we were a missionary or really unlucky.

As a Catholic, you were taught to contemplate your last end. You were encouraged to rehearse, in advance, your own death: with its accompanying agonies of mind and body, and (I found this a homely touch) your friends and relations hovering about your bed.

It is true that the 'Litany for a Happy Death' didn't form part of the prayers I was taught in school. But at eight or nine years old, bored with the unvarying form of Holy Mass, and in despair of hearing a good sermon, I used to thumb through to the back of the prayer book.

O Lord Jesus, God of goodness and Father of mercies, I draw nigh to thee with a contrite and humble heart; to Thee I recommend the last hour of my life, and that judgement which awaits me afterwards.

When my feet, benumbed with death, shall admonish me that my mortal course is drawing to an end, *Merciful Jesus, have mercy on me.*

When my hands, cold and trembling, shall no

longer be able to clasp the crucifix, and, against
my will shall let it fall on my bed of suffering,
Merciful Jesus, have mercy on me.

When my eyes, dim and troubled at the
approach of death, shall fix themselves on Thee,
my last and only support, *Merciful Jesus, have
mercy on me.*

When my lips, pale and trembling, shall pronounce for the last time Thine adorable name,
Merciful Jesus, have mercy on me.

I take death as serious and proximate, I always have.
But recently, when a doctor asked for my family
history, I had to knock him back on every score.
No heart disease. No strokes. No cancer: except for
Grandad, and he was a smoker. No reason, in fact (I
said this wonderingly, raising my face) no reason, it
seems, we should ever die.

But the litany tells us we will, and how it will
look:

When my face, pale and livid, shall inspire the
beholders with pity and dismay; when my hair,
bathed in the sweat of death, and stiffening on my
head, shall forebode my approaching end, *Merciful
Jesus, have mercy on me.*

When mine ears, soon to be for ever shut to
the discourse of men, shall be open to hear the

irrevocable decree, which is to fix my doom for
all eternity, *Merciful Jesus, have mercy on me.*

When my imagination, agitated by dreadful
spectres –

But no, perhaps I have agitated you enough. I admire
particularly the phrase about the hair stiffening on
the head. This road to dissolution, the good Catholic
was encouraged to walk regularly, following Christ to
Calvary. St Peter, we were taught, was crucified upside
down; this was more merciful for him, since he would
have lost consciousness. I was told this three times
during my high school education, by the same woman,
and each time in my mind I rehearsed her solemn
upending, as if she were a geometrical figure that I
had been asked to envisage in some other position. I
think she believed Peter had got off lightly.

When the last tear, the forerunner of my dissolution, shall drop from mine eyes, receive it as a
sacrifice of expiation for my sins; grant that I may
expire the victim of penance, and in that dreadful
moment, *Merciful Jesus, have mercy on me.*

Note that excellent semicolon. People ask how I
learned to write. That's where I learned it.

The whole of a Catholic life is lived in the shadow
of the happy death – as if your life were to be

enacted through a silvered, speckled mirror, ancient and flattering.

La la la. Ma ma ma. December 1979: I felt the urge to leave a note by my bed: if I wake up a vegetable, put me in a stew.

When I was half awake, a day later, they came to tell me what they had done. After a general anaesthetic, you dip in and out of consciousness: sitting up and smiling, you may be the picture of alertness, but your attention has faded. They should have told me again, I think, when I was properly awake. They should have told me once or twice. They should have written me a letter, they should have written me an essay or maybe a small book.

Certain things were over for me now. I sensed it would not be easy to shore up my collapsing marriage. When women apes have their wombs removed, and are returned by keepers to the community, their mates sense it, and desert them. It is a fact of base biology; there is little kindness in the animal kingdom, and I had been down there with the animals, grunting and bleeding on the porter's trolley. There would be no daughter, no Catriona; not that I could claim I had wanted her too hard; at twenty-seven I hadn't ever tried to have a baby. We seemed fine as we were, the two of us. 'The children of lovers are orphans,' said

Robert Louis Stevenson. That would have been a sad fate for her, little Miss Cat. She would never be born now, and we were no longer lovers.

I was missing a few bits of me, besides my womb and ovaries, my reproductive apparatus. A few lengths of bowel: but you've plenty to spare.

Do you know what worries me most about this memoir? That I'm always the smart one. Always the one with the last word. Always the one with the heartless quip, the derisive bon mot.

But now I had to reckon with this: I hadn't been smart at all. Like a cretin, like some dumb little angel, I had believed what I was told. I believed that the pains which ran through my body each month were part of the burden of womanhood. I didn't say to my doctors, by the way, my menstrual periods are agony. I thought they would say, get away, you, little Miss Neverwell! And when I had, timidly, approached the topic, they'd said robustly, whoah, now, you don't want to worry! Period pains? That'll clear up, my dear, after you have your first baby. Just you wait and see!

I was brought up as a Catholic and it's not easy to throw over the faith. I believed that, short of crucifixion, you shouldn't really complain.

I was quickly out of bed. I tried to persuade the surgeons to let me go early, but they wouldn't. One of the girls on the ward had got a make-up kit for Christmas, and told me to help myself to it. I thought we should have our faces on, to meet 1980, so though I wasn't very upright, because of my stitches, I painted us, young and old. Even Elsie, who was eighty-three, blushed beneath her blusher when I held up the hand mirror so she could see my work. 'Look at me,' she said, 'Is that me? I've never worn rouge!'

For the rest of us I painted deep kohl eyes and ruby lips. The Senior Registrar came in and caught me crouching over my patient. 'Oh, you girls,' he said, laughing. He walked away, chuckling happily to himself: another bunch of happy punters.

Oh, you girls! What are you like?

The incision ran up the midline of my body, slashed from pubic bone to navel.

About four months later, after repeated courses of penicillin had got me over the infections that I had contracted while in the hospital, I returned to Botswana, to my ailing marriage, my house, my dogs and cats. I am going to be better now, I said, I am going to be different. I went back to the GP who had been treating me, or failing to treat me: downtown, the dusty consulting room under the eucalyptus trees. I found it hard to talk; I thought I had nothing to be ashamed of, but somehow I felt ashamed, and I was not sure how confidential was my consultation; secrets did seem to leak, in this small bush town. I told him about the surgery, shuffling my feet. 'So,' I said, 'you see, in the end, it turned out there wasn't much to be done, by the stage I'd reached. It turned out a bit of a catastrophe.'

'Oh well,' he said. He shuffled his own sandalled feet under his desk. 'There's one good thing, anyway. Now you won't have to worry about birth prevention.'

I had been, until Christmas, a woman who thought she had a choice. I was twenty-seven and I thought I could have a baby, even if I didn't want one, even if my husband didn't; I was free in the matter, there were possibilities. Now I was not free and the possibilities were closed off. Biology was destiny. Neglect – my own, and that of the medical profession – had taken away my choices. Now my body was not my own. It was a thing done to, a thing operated on. I was twenty-seven and an old woman, all at once. I had undergone what is called a 'surgical menopause' or what textbooks of the time called 'female castration'. I was a eunuch, then? Castration is a punishment; what was my crime? It used to be fashionable to call endometriosis 'the career woman's disease': the implication being, there now, you callous bitch, see what you get if you put off breeding and put your own ambitions first. I was no good for breeding, so what was I good for? Who was I at all? My hormonal circuits were busted, my endocrinology was shot to pieces. I was old while I was young, I was an ape, I was a blot on the page, I was a nothing, zilch. The publisher had turned down my French Revolution book. It seemed I couldn't even write. But come now – let's break open the champagne! At least I won't have to worry about birth prevention!

There are times in life when you are justified in punching someone in the face. But I didn't react. I knew it was for the doctor to direct the blow, and me to absorb it. Sometimes one takes a little pride in endurance of this kind. At that stage it was all that was left.

When I left St George's Hospital, I imagined that aspects of my past had been excised, cut cleanly away. My long scar would knit and the memory of the pain would fade. For a time I went to and fro, between England and Africa, and in the end I tried to put down roots in the colder climate, and make my way alone. But by 1982 I was sick again, pain slicing through my vital organs and leaving me breathless in public places, leaning against a grimy wall at Euston Station, or clinging like a derelict to a park bench. My skin turned grey, and my weight began to fall, so that one day, when I saw myself sideways through a mirror, I shocked myself: I looked like one of those beaten dogs that the RSPCA used to photograph, with bones sticking through the hide. I hadn't known that the endometriosis could come back.

Though it is true that radical surgery is usually a cure for the condition, it is also the case that it is difficult to eradicate every misplaced cell, to pick off those minute guerrilla fighters waging a long war in the obscure cavities of the body. The hormone oestrogen, like fresh supplies and *matériel*, allows the guerrillas to flourish. I didn't know that then. If I didn't take oestrogen replacement, I had been told, my bones would crumble. How much to take? No one seemed to know. Trial and error, I was told breezily. Take enough so that you don't get the symptoms of the menopause.

Soon I was suffering almost continuous pain. Ignorant doctors whom I encountered told me the disease could not return. The pain was the pull of scar tissue, adhesions, or if it wasn't that, then once again I was imagining things. This should have made me angry, but I was too fragile and worn to react as I should. There was little information available to the public, no support groups in those days. When I found a doctor who believed in my problem and was prepared to treat me, my reaction was only gratitude.

The treatment was drugs now, hormones. The first weeks were tough. On a summer's day, wrapped in a big quilt, my teeth chattered as they had in Africa when I had contracted dysentery. But the tropical infection had left me light and hollow; now, I seemed to be gaining flesh. I entered treatment weighing something over seven and a half stone. By the end of nine months, which was the usual duration of the course, the pain was no better, but my bodyweight had increased by over fifty per cent and was rising.

When I gained the first stone or two, I didn't really mind. If you are secure in one aspect of your appearance – and there had never been anything to quibble about, with my shape – you don't mind small changes, they don't seem threatening, and in fact they give you a chance to alter your style. I'd always been afraid of showing my arms, in case people thought I was from the Third World and gave me a donation; and my upper ribs, I'd always thought, looked somewhat tubercular. It was good that I looked healthier; I was tired of people asking what was wrong with me, and giving me those dirty looks that very thin women get all the time. I'd even been turned down for a job, by a broad-beamed horse-faced woman who said I looked weak; other jobs had been barred to me as soon as my medical record was discovered. It was a bit like going back to the nineteen seventies. In those days, interviewers looked sourly at me because I was married, and looked fertile; so why didn't they like me any better, now I was on my own and incapable of childbearing?

At nine stone and size twelve, graceful and cur-
vaceous, I got a job. It was quite a menial one, so I got
another, for the evenings. One job was in a shop, the
other in a bar. The jobs needed a sort of uniform, so I
bought some cheap black skirts and white tops. Within
a couple of weeks I had grown out of them. My face
was round and looked childish; I was becoming like
some phenomenal baby, who astounds her attendants.
When my next appointment with my consultant came,
I said, I'm worried because I'm putting on weight so
fast. She shot me a spiteful glance, from amid her own
jowly folds. Now, she said, you know what it's like for
the rest of us.

I found a second-hand shop quite near where I
lived; it sold cast-offs from the bored, with the odd
designer label. I was determined not to panic, but I
stopped eating, of course; what else could I do? In any
case, my body was staging some kind of revolt; colic,
nausea, an inability to keep food inside me. To get out
of the house for eight, I had to get up at six. I spent my
scarce free time getting my hair done, lifted and teased
and curled into a mane, so that I didn't look as if I had
a pin-head on top of my sweetly plump shoulders. I was
a size fourteen for a while, and people would say, 'You
look so *well* – been away somewhere nice, have you?'

My ex-husband came back from Africa. He had
once told me that I was so vain of my waistline that
I would starve rather than gain an inch. But how did

he know? In the past it had never been an issue. Now I had starved, and still gained five. Not to worry! He took me shopping. I bought some Englishwomen's dresses, the pretty, floppy kind that go with creamy skin and broad haunches. We got married again. I had warned him by letter that I was fat now, but I knew I was being melodramatic. Size fourteen's not fat, not really, it's just – it's *well*. That's what it is. *Well*.

I never was a size sixteen. I shot past it effortlessly. Soon there was nothing in the second-hand shop to fit me; bigger women don't discard fashions so lightly. The assistants – and hadn't I been their best customer all summer? – began to give me the smirk, half-commiserating and half-condescending, that would soon become the usual expression of shop girls when I went to get clad. My skin turned grey, shading to slate-blue as the autumn came on. My legs swelled and ached. Fluid puffed up my eyelids. Some mornings my head looked like a soccer ball. I was glad when my husband's job took us to Saudi Arabia, where women wear drapery rather than clothes, and where no one knew me, so that no one could stop me in the street to say how *well* I looked; where, in fact, I was more or less prohibited from going out on the street at all. I could stay indoors, under artificial light, waxing like some strange fungus.

The failure of my drugs had been recognised, and before I left England I was put on a new type. By now I was not so green in judgement. I looked up the side effects. Weight gain – I'd done that, and I didn't think there were sizes bigger than twenty: not really, not for people who'd once been thin. Hair falls out. Well, I had plenty of hair. Voice deepens – never mind, I'd always been a squeaker. Spots – harder to put a good face on spots, but never mind, the clued-up woman knows how to cope with a little outbreak. A general virilisation . . . oh, what's the odds? I'd always wanted to be a bloke.

A few weeks on, I had developed a steroid moon-face. My hair had come out in handfuls. I was deaf, my eyesight was blurred by constant headaches, and my legs were swollen like bolsters. And one morning I sat up in bed, and cried out, like a nude exposed in a comic strip, *eek!* I clapped my outstretched palms where my breasts had been, and there they weren't anymore.

Then I had a bit of luck. I needed a prescription, and a doctor's letter; my new drugs would have to be sent for from England, as they were not available in Saudi Arabia. I swayed, giddy and wincing, into a doctor's office. Let me name him – why not? His name was Dr Fishlock. He sat up at the sight of me, and asked 'What are you taking?' He fixed me with a keen look, of knowledge and concern. I told him. It confirmed what he had suspected. He knew the drug, he said. He had worked on the clinical trials. It was effective: but but but.

I knew the buts. I was a walking but. A butt of ridicule, in my own eyes; a sad sack enclosing a disease process, no longer an object of respect, or self-respect. He spoke to me kindly, and cut the dose by a third.

Very few doctors understand this: that somehow, you have to live till you're cured.

I went home, to the dark, enclosed rooms of our city apartment. I cut my dose by a third. Bald, odd-shaped, deaf but not defeated, I sat down and wrote another book.

When I was thin I had no notion of what being fat is like. When I worked in a department store I had sold clothes to women of most sizes, so I should have known; but perhaps you have to experience the state from the inside, to understand what fat is like. When you sell clothes you get very good at sizing people, but I had sized my customers as if they were fridge-freezers, or some other unnegotiable object, solid and with a height, width and depth. Fat is not like this. It is insidious and creepy. It is not a matter of chest-waist-hip measurement. You get fat knees, fat feet, fat in bits of you that you'd never thought of. You get in a panic, and believe in strange diets; you give up carbohydrate, then fat, then you subsist for a bit on breakfast cereal and fruit because it seems easier that way; then you find yourself weak at the fat knees, at risk of falling over in the street. You get up on winter mornings to pack ice cubes into a diet shake that tastes like some imbibed jelly, a primitive life form that will bud inside you. You throw tantrums in fat-lady shops, where the stock is grimy tat tacked together from cheap man-made fabric, choice of electric blue or cerise. You can't get your legs into boots, or your feet into last year's shoes.

You say, OK, then I'll be fat. As it seems you have no choice, you generously concur. But you become a little wary of adverbs like 'generously'. Of adjectives like 'full-bodied', 'womanly' or 'ample'. You think people are staring at you, talking about you. They probably are. One of my favoured grim sports, since I became a published writer and had people to interview me, has been to wait and see how the profiler will turn me out in print. With what adjective will they characterise the startlingly round woman on whose sofa they are lolling? 'Apple-cheeked' is the sweetest. 'Maternal' made me smile: well, almost.

OK, you say, it seems I can't be thin, so I'll be fat and make the best of it. 'Fat is a Feminist Issue,' you tell yourself. Fat is not immoral. There is no link between your waistline and your ethics. But though you insist on this, in your own mind, everything tells you you're wrong; or, let's say, you're going in for a form of intellectual discrimination that cuts against the perception of most of the population, who know that overweight people are lazy, undisciplined slobs. Their perception, of course, is conditioned, not natural. The ancient prejudice in favour of fat has reversed only recently. When I taught in African schools, the high school girls thought slimness was a prize to be gained by hard study. As soon as their certificates allowed them to get away from mealie-porridge, the diet of their foremothers, they planned to turn svelte. But poor girls, without certificates, whom I met at my volunteer project, were aiming only to get as much mealie-porridge as the high school students. 'Tell me about your best friend,' I urged my little maids one day. 'Now, write it down. Two sentences, can you?' My star pupil leaned against me, in friendly local style, while she read her composition. Her exercise book flopped in my lap, one sinewy arm was thrown across my shoulders. Her other hand trailed towards the book, her finger stabbed at the words: 'My beast friend is Neo. It is a beautiful girl, and fat.'

I think of her sometimes, my beast friend. In the terms of the church in which I was brought up, the body is a beast, a base, simian relative that turns up at the door of the spirit too often for comfort; a bawling uncle, drunk, who raps with the door knocker and sings in the street. Saints starve. They diet till they see visions. Sometimes they see the towers of the fortresses of God, the battlements outlined in flickering light. They are haunted by strange odours:

heavenly perfumes, or diabolic stenches. Sometimes they have to rise from their pallets and kick their demons out. Some saints are muscular Christians. But there are no fat saints.

When you get fat, you get a new personality. You can't help it. Complete strangers ascribe it to you. When I was thin and quick on my feet, a girl with a head of blonde hair, I went for weeks without a kind word. But why would I need one? When I grew fat, I was assumed to be placid. I was the same strung-out fired-up person I'd always been, but to the outward eye I had acquired serenity. A whole range of maternal virtues were ascribed to me. I was (and am) unsure about how I am related to my old self, or to myself from year to year. The hormonal profile of an individual determines much of the manifest personality. If you skew the endocrine system, you lose the pathways to self. When endocrine patterns change it alters the way you think and feel. One shift in the pattern tends to trip another.

Some time about the millennium, I stopped being able to think properly. I lost my capacity for snappy summation, and my sense of priorities went too, so that when I was writing I would dwell on minor points at great length, while failing to get around to the main point at all. I could start things, but not finish them. I had no appetite, but grew still wider. Sleep became my only interest. In the end, it was discovered that my thyroid gland had failed. A simple pill treats it; your brain works again, but your body is slower to catch up. Nowadays, more than twenty years on from my trip to St George's Hospital, everything about me – my physiology, my psychology – feels constantly under assault: I am a shabby old building in an area of heavy shelling, which the inhabitants have vacated years ago.

I am not writing to solicit any special sympathy. People survive much worse and never put pen to paper. I am writing in order to take charge of the story of my childhood and my childlessness; and in order to locate myself, if not within a body, then in the narrow space between one letter and the next, between the lines where the ghosts of meaning are. Spirit needs a house and lodges where it can; you don't kill yourself, just because you need loose covers rather than frocks. There are other people who, like me, have had the roots of their personality torn up. You need to find yourself, in the maze of social expectation, the thickets of memory: just which bits of you are left intact? I have been so mauled by medical procedures, so sabotaged and made over, so thin and so fat, that sometimes I feel that each morning it is necessary to write myself into being – even if the writing is aimless doodling that no one will ever read, or the diary that no one can see till I'm dead. When you have committed enough words to paper you feel you have a spine stiff enough to stand up in the wind. But when you stop writing you find that's all you are, a spine, a row of rattling vertebrae, dried out like an old quill pen.

When you were a child you had to create yourself from whatever was to hand. You had to construct yourself and make yourself into a person, fitting somehow into the niche that in your family has been always vacant, or into a vacancy left by someone dead. Sometimes you looked towards dead man's shoes, seeing how, in time, you would replace your grandmother, or her elder sister, or someone who no one really remembered but who ought to have been there: someone's miscarriage, someone's dead child. Much of what happened to you, in your early life, was constructed inside your head. You were a passive observer, you were the done-to, you were the not-explained-to; you had to listen at doors for information, or sometimes it was what you overheard; but just as often it was disinformation, or half a tale, and much of the time you probably put the wrong construction on what you picked up. How then can you create a narrative of your own life? Janet Frame compares the process to finding a bunch of old rags, and trying to make a dress. A party dress, I'd say: something fit to be seen in. Something to go out in and face the world.

For a few years, in my dreams, I stayed thin, and I wore a thin person's clothes. Even today, I sometimes see myself, in one of the cities I go to when I am asleep, coming out of a bookshop or sitting at a café table, trim and narrow, though younger than I am now. It is said that, in dreams – in a lucid dream, where you are aware of your own processes – you can't turn on an electric light, or see yourself in a mirror. I set myself to test this; thinking that somehow, if I could see my fat self in a dream, I would have accepted it all through, and would accept the waking reality.

But what happens, when you face the mirror, is that its surface melts, and the self walks into the glass. You step through it, and into a different dream.

It was 1982 when I went to Saudi Arabia; I was thirty. The expatriate wives of Jeddah plagued the life out of me, sticking me like mosquitoes with their common question: 'When are you going to start your family?'

I didn't know what was a good answer to this: I'm not, or I can't.

When I was a young woman I didn't want children. I was wary of the trap that seemed ready to spring. I was ambitious, on my own account, to make a mark on the world. I didn't want to carry someone else's thwarted expectations. If I failed to make something of myself, wouldn't I heap my frustration on to my daughter? And she, in course of time, on to her daughter? When is it a woman's turn, I wanted to know, to get something for herself, and not at second hand through her children? I was good for more than breeding: that was my opinion.

But my opinion faltered, in the face of the expat matrons smelling so sweetly of baby talc and cream. It was hard to tell them that I had turned my back on everything that gave life meaning for them, turned my back until it was too late for me. Once it was necessary for my husband's employer to arrange for my drugs to be brought in by courier, the rumour got about that they were fertility drugs. 'They can do wonders nowadays,' I was assured. Eyes were on my waistline; which was, of course, ever-expanding. After the natural gestation period had passed, the ladies gossiped among themselves that I was trying to adopt.

This made me angry; after a bit, it made me laugh. Would any agency have thought me a suitable adoptive mother? Adoption agencies don't like sick women for parents. And why would I want a child not my own? I needed to reflect my glorious ancestry. My forebear who crushed a riot, who was made a sanitary inspector. My great-grandmother, who liked a drink but never smoked a pipe. My great-grandfather, who built a wall an army could have marched on.

I should have been a 'schoolgirl mother', I thought: that social scourge. At fourteen I might have been fertile. At seventeen. But after that – I have to read my pain backwards, to know what was happening inside me – I guess my chances were decreasing. Those crippling spasms that had to be ignored, those deep aches with no name, those washes of nausea, were not evidence of a neurotic personality, or of my ambivalence about my gender, and they were not brought on by 'nerves', or by fear of failure in a man's world. They were evidence of a pathological process that would destroy the chance of my having a child and land me with chronic ill health. I wonder why, despite all, I did not insist, could not insist, that doctors paid attention to me and located my malaise. There are several possible explanations, on several levels. One is that, in the time and place where I grew up, expectations of health were low, especially for women. The proper attitude to doctors was humble gratitude; you cleaned the house before they arrived. The deeper explanation is that I always felt that I deserved very little, that I would probably not be happy in life, and that the safest thing was to lie down and die. The reasons for this elude me now. I wish I could explain them better and make them add up. But we were always told at school, when tackling a sum, to 'show your workings'. Even if you didn't get the answer right, we were told, you might get the odd mark for honest effort.

What I would have liked was a choice in life. Leisure, to reverse my earlier decision that children didn't matter to me; leisure, to ask if circumstances or my mind had changed. No one can predict that the game will be over for them at the age of twenty-seven.

The time I fell in love is the time I should have acted, and now that an era of my life is over, and my schoolfriends are becoming grandmothers, I miss the child I never had. I know what Catriona would have been like. I have a mental picture of her, which I have built like one of those criminal profilers whose formulations – let's be honest – never fit too well. She would be nothing like me at all. She would be strong like my mother, broad-shouldered like my husband, with that milky Irish skin that freckles but never tans. I see her small competent hands, chopping an onion; making unwritten dishes, which she has never been taught to make. She would manage her money well, and perhaps manage other people's; perhaps that's how she'd make a living. She would drive a car, and sing in tune, and know about things like making curtains, which have always defeated me.

People romance about their children long before they are born – long before, and long after. They name them and rename them. They see them as their second chances, 'a chance to get it right this time', as if they were able to give birth to themselves. They have children to compensate themselves for the things they didn't do or didn't get in their own early life. They conceive because they feel impelled to make up, to a non-existent person, for a loss they themselves have suffered. Children are born because their parents feel the defects in themselves, and want to mend them;

or because they are bored; or because they feel that in some mysterious way it is time for children, and that if they don't have them their lives will begin to leak meaning away. Some women have babies to give a present to their own mother, or to prove themselves her equal. Motives are seldom simple and never pure. Children are never simply themselves, co-extensive with their own bodies, becoming alive to us when they turn in the womb, or with their first unaided breath. Their lives start long before birth, long before conception, and if they are aborted or miscarried or simply fail to materialise at all, they become ghosts within our lives.

Women who have miscarried know this, of course, but so does any woman who has ever suspected herself to be pregnant when she wasn't. It's impossible not to calculate, if I *had* been, it would have been born, let's see, in November, ice on the roads, early dark; it would have been the offspring of late March, a child of uncertain sun and squalls. No doubt there are ghosts within the lives of men; a man with daughters brings his son into being through wishing him, as a man somehow better than himself, and a father of sons wraps his unborn daughter in swaddling bands and guards her virginity, like an unspoiled realm of himself. Even adulterers have their ghost children. Illicit lovers say: what would *our* child be like? Then, when they have parted or are forced apart, the child goes on growing up, a shadow, a half-shadow of possibility. The country of the unborn is criss-crossed by the roads not taken, the paths we turned our back on. In a sly state of half-becoming, they lurk in the shadowland of chances missed.

I never saw a ghost in Africa, though more than once death came so near me I had to grapple with him. It seemed to me that ghosts – the knocking, echoing, pesky sort – were a manifestation of Europe that would trail after the person who was not yet at home in Africa: who was only half-adjusted to a new, deeper state of emergency. I never felt that unease in the empty house, the queasiness of populated rooms where you can't see the population: or fear of the dark. It seemed to me that symbols in Africa organised themselves differently. Outward manifestation of inner chaos came in fatal road accidents and suicides: the truck without lights, the one drink too many, the mis-spelled police report that got filed in the waste bin. Any number of lives were trashed, casually, born and unborn; and in Africa, I actually knew a woman who died in childbirth. She was just one among the continent's casualties, but the one I used to speak to every day. I didn't like her much, in fact; I'd like to say I mourned, but it would be stretching a point.

Jeddah was different. My life in Saudi Arabia, for at

least two years, was like life in gaol. Simple force of will – or the force of simple will – could move the furniture and rip off the wardrobe doors. At times of stress, or on the brink of change, you can seem to act as a conduit for whatever disorganised, irrational forces are in the air. Shut in those dark rooms, life going on elsewhere, my body subject to strange mutations, I accumulated an anger that would rip a roof off.

When I came back to England, and gave up my concealing Islamic draperies, neighbourly eyes would note my bulk and ask, when is your baby due? Sometimes kindly women, waiting on a station bench, would edge along for me. Once, a young Scots boy, too new to London to have lost his natural grace, offered me his seat on the tube and, because I felt so ill, I thanked him with an astonished smile, and sat on it. The unborn, whether they're named or not, whether or not they're acknowledged, have a way of insisting: a way of making their presence felt. No advance in medical technology was going to produce Catriona; she was lost. But when biological destiny veers from the norm, there are parts of the psyche that take time to catch up. You understand what has happened, the medical disaster; you reason about it. But there are layers of realisation, and a feeling of loss takes time to sink through those layers. The body is not logical; it knows its own mad pathways. Mourning is not quick; when there is no body to bury, mourning is not final. I used to say (because flippancy was my weapon) look, it's a good thing I never had children, because I'd be putting them outside the door while I finished a paragraph; I'd be saying, don't you know I've this piece to do for the newspaper, why don't you go and play in the road? No more sombre enemy of good art than the pram in the hall: did Connolly ever write a truer word?

But at a less conscious level, I kept on planning for Catriona: for her brothers, and for their children too. This is the only conclusion I can reach, when I look at the strange decisions I took about real estate in the late eighties, the nineties. Property was a sound investment, of course, but I think I had investments that went beyond the financial. The larders were stocked with food, the presses with sheets. We could have provisioned a small army from the stuff that was stacked in the garages. After we bought Owl Cottage, we had accumulated a total of seven bedrooms, four lavatories, a duplication of domestic machines, the capacity to wash clothes for eight people at once, to do the dishes for sixteen. Who did I think was coming, unless the unborn; or possibly the dead? The hungry family of uncles, wanting ham and Cheshire cheese: their own dead offspring, that missing generation: my own missing daughter trailing her offspring, a green-eyed girl with my green-eyed grandchildren. What's to be done with the lost, the dead, but write them into being?

There is a certain pathos attached to ghosts, to household sprites and those hobgoblins that jump into the vision between waking and sleep. At one time, I was plagued by a spate of dreams in which I was a midwife who had let a child die; but when I got my first book on track again, and when, after many years in limbo, it was published at last, those dreams ceased. But time goes on, you think of more and more books you should have written, stories half-fledged and left in the file called 'Work in Progress'. I know some of these narratives will never be finished. I dream of half-formed, foetal beings, left abandoned on a cold floor. Sometimes they are blackened, like frozen corpses. They take malign forms: I dream of a castle floor, where the children come shrieking through, and so evil are they, that they have the actual capacity of revolting stone, of making the flags shrink away from them. Risen from the ground, they are naked and sexless, foul-mouthed and knowing. My impulse is to injure or kill them, swat them like flies, like little demons that, if they're left, will range about the world and will bad-mouth me and misrepresent me and filch from me everything I have.

But then I wake up, chilled, and put out my hands to be sure that surfaces are solid, that my own flesh is still warm. I grope for a pen and write down my dream; when the day has settled around me, the prosaic Surrey light, I take my dream to the keyboard and mince it through a second draft.

Afterlife

When we came home from Saudi Arabia, we
had various houses. Some of them had minor
poltergeists, and one of them was home to a nebu-
lous cat. People less suggestible than me were aware
of these anomalous phenomena, rational people who
didn't make their living by what they could conjure up;
so I feel it's all right to admit that I gave houseroom to
some ghosts. Ghosts are the tags and rags of everyday
life, information you acquire that you don't know what
to do with, knowledge that you can't process; they're
cards thrown out of your card index, blots on the page.
'Ghosts' are whatever it is that moves the furniture,
stops the clocks, hides things from you and arranges
for you to be locked out of your hotel room. It's just
the little dead, I say to myself, kicking up a fuss,
demanding attention by the infantile methods that
are the only ones available to them.

We lived first in a tiny flat in Windsor, the castle
looming in at the window. Then, to buy space, in a no
man's land along an arterial road, somewhere outside

Slough. At the time we bought Owl Cottage we were living in Sunningdale in a ramshackle flat converted from a former mother and baby home, which had been run by nuns.

Drummond House was built of a red brick whose colour time didn't soften. By the look of it, it had been put up in the 1890s, with 1920s additions. Its façade was blunt, square and ugly; the back of the building was tile-hung, like an overgrown cottage, and almost had charm. After the place had been hacked into flats, there were four households under the one roof, and a poor sort of roof it was; when it rained we had to run around with buckets. The big rooms were gracelessly partitioned, and there were crucifixes and Latin mottoes in unexpected places, and one of the neighbours was spiteful and intractably litigious. But there were compensations; a copper beech behind the house filtered into the rooms, on winter afternoons, a lemon-coloured light, and as you lay in the deep Edwardian bathtub, you could hear in the background the reassuring shuffle of branch-line trains. In summer there was a backcloth of shifting, rustling green, green against green, as if the whole world were made of leaves.

We had been seven years in this house. Then, within the space of a few months, it became unbearable. It was a wasting asset, its lease shortening. We decided to sell up to a builder, who would give us the market rate for the flat in return for our deposit on a patch of rutted ground eight miles away, ground on which stood, preconceived but not yet embryonic, a five-bed detached 'executive home'.

We had looked at the plans of the 'executive homes' with fewer bedrooms, but they were dispiriting hutches. 'We'll go for the biggest one,' we said: five beds and three baths. I can have two offices, I thought, in two of the bedrooms. And think; a spare room with the beds made up tidily, where guests will be en-suite and always expected: instead of this ambling around in the small hours with a drink in one hand, a pillowcase in the other, a towel over your shoulder and the guest trailing behind you, bleating, 'Don't go to any trouble.' And we'll have a garden that will be – unlike our garden in Sunningdale – attached to the house. And think of the central heating – our own modern controllable system, instead of the monster boiler of Drummond House, housed in its own shed or cave, which demanded each autumn the sacrifice of seven virgins before it would agree to splutter into life and infiltrate a vitiating heat between the whistling draughts.

We spent a nervous summer, thinking that the litigious neighbour would somehow spoil this happy arrangement. In the evenings, we drove over to the building site, where down the hillside spilled walls grown to the height of eight-year-olds. These walls, soon, would be raised up; one evening we stood under the vast gaping skeleton of the roof, looking up at its timbers, arched above us like the ribs of a brontosaurus. On later visits, we climbed into the pre-rooms, and looked out through the holes where windows would be. We would see other couples, picking their way through the caterpillar tracks in the churned-up earth, between the pipes and cables; we would see the wondering look in their eyes. No one could believe that out of these bits of plastic and concrete the vast solid structures would grow, the structures of family houses, houses for the stable modern families of Middle England.

They were not, our neighbours-to-be, the kind of families whom the break-up statistics comprehend. They were not the sort for adulterous upsets, for drunken fumbles, for spring *folie*, for subterfuge and lies. They were grounded infotec folk, hardware or software people, bright philistines, sharp and intelligent. They were mobile in their habits till their children fixed them; keen, pragmatic, willing to defer gratification; committed to their offspring, investing in them. Men and wives met each other halfway, gentle fathers and defined, energetic mothers. They were a new sort of people who didn't seem to feel the need of history, personal or collective. They seemed to have sprung straight from a pot in Homebase, putting out glossy, polished leaves; they had parents, but they had them as weekend accessories, appearing on summer Sundays like their barbecue forks. In this part of the world each family unit runs like a model small business, and the accounts, you may be sure, are squared at the end of each quarter; and if quarter is wanted, a small measure is granted; and if quarter is granted, the favour must be returned; and when the columns are totted they must balance, I think, husband to wife, wife to husband, with none of the shocking deficits that are incurred in the wilder parts of the world.

One evening we drove up to the site and saw that they were putting the façade on our executive home. The drawings had lied to us; we had not been promised this. For some time we sat in our parked car. I may have used some rough language, and said I wanted out of the deal. But my sentiments dried on the air. It was too late. We were committed. After all, I said at last, when you're in it, you don't have to look at it, do you?

We moved in November. They were someone else's problem, the half-timbered elevations from Disneyland, the herringbone 'brickwork' that was as thick as cardboard, glued on to the raw building blocks beneath: the fake leaded windows. Our problems, the builders told us brightly, were just what you call 'snagging', for instance, the central heating that creaked and banged, and groaned in the night like a ghoul. Once we had settled in, we were able to relax and appreciate the house's more charming features. The washbasins were specially designed so that the soap slid off them, unless you wedged it behind the tap. The watered-down paint on the walls was so thin that a casual wipe with a cloth would remove it, along with the mark that had offended you.

Summer came. The newly turfed gardens sprouted a mini-estate of multicoloured Wendy houses and play shacks, plastic slides and swings and paddling pools. I should like to say that the happy laughter of children drifted in from the gardens, but more often it was their aggrieved wails as they pitched off their climbing frames head first, or were beaten up by their brothers and sisters. As I sat in my stifling upstairs room, coaxing out of my computer the novel concealed somewhere in its operating system, I could hear their mothers' voices from below, running the gamut from coaxing to shrieks of fury. I asked myself, why don't they like their children more? Why are they so angry with them for doing childish things? If they hate childhood so much, why didn't they arrange to give birth to adults?

For a year or two in the new house, our possessions expanded to fill the rooms. The cupboards were packed with linen and towels. We bought everything by the

dozen. We had bath cleaner by the crate: enough sandwich bags for a primary school picnic: enough tinfoil to
wrap a town hall. Shuttling to and fro between Surrey
and Norfolk required lists, master-lists and sub-lists,
and constant calculation and re-calculation of stocks
and supplies. Was everything scrubbed and scoured?
Was everything warm? Was every cupboard full to
capacity, and everything scraped up to the standard
that – God knows why – I had set myself? My
husband knew a couple, childless like us, who ate
out every night. They kept nothing in their fridge
but a bottle of champagne and an inch of souring
milk. Imagine, I thought, any woman so deficient
in household arts; imagine any man, so wretchedly
deprived of pies. Myself, I never peeled two pounds
of potatoes if I thought five would do. I would take
up two great fistfuls of spaghetti and toss them in
the boiling pot. I used to think, there's plenty here,
for anybody who drops in.

There must have been a moment of realisation,
though I don't remember it clearly: a moment when
I looked at the contents of the cupboards and said,
but who is all this for? Who am I expecting? I knew,
if I thought about it, that I was expecting the unborn.
But could I face them, any more? Perhaps I'd grown
away from them, without noticing it, over the years.
One day, when I was upstairs in one of my two offices,
listening to my best bit of Telemann, the merry,

jingling ice-cream van lurched around the corner: 'Today's the day the teddy bears have their picnic.'

I left my desk and fell into my armchair; a chair which (like many of our chairs) could be pulled out to form a spare bed. Bugger off teddy bears, I said: hugging myself, my head drooping. I had always thought that song was sinister: 'If you go down to the woods today you're in for a big surprise.' I was angry, unreasonably so. I felt I had been invaded by the juvenile, my attention trashed. What would I do if real children came padding at the door, smiling their sticky smiles, smearing my printout with sticky hands and pressing 'delete' on my keyboard? I could have coped once, of course; I'd have found a way to laugh about it. I'd have said they were my inspiration, that I'd be only half a woman without them. But that was *then*, when I was twenty-five, in the days when, notionally anyway, I was fertile. Now I was tired, more fragile, less tolerant. I stood up, closed the window, put the Telemann on again and sat down at my desk.

Then a thing occurred to me, about ghost children. They don't age, unless you make them. They don't age, so they don't know it's time to leave home. They won't, without a struggle, be kicked out of your psyche. They will hang on by every means they know; they won't agree to go, until you make your intentions very clear. They're stupid, so it's not enough to tell them; you have to show them as well.

I went round to my next-door neighbour. 'You know you said, if we were ever selling the house, that we should tell you before we told anyone else?'

Oh, wow, said my neighbour. You're going, are you?

Come over, I said, when the children get home. Have a look around. Think where everything would go. At four o'clock they came in a gang. The children whooped through the rooms. They couldn't wait to evict us. Only the three-year-old sobbed, 'When do we swap the pets?' for she thought that we were exchanging houses and all their contents, and that she had to give up her white rabbit for the cat who was steadily hating her from a bookshelf, thinking which way to prey on her would be best. Once we knew her mistake, we soon ironed it out, soothed her temper. That evening, over a bottle of wine, we shook hands on the deal. Our 'second home' must go as well, we decide. If we're going to remake our lives, we must do the job properly.

It is 12 August, 2000: a Sunday in Norfolk. We are taking Owl Cottage apart. My elder brother and my husband carry out the pine table, which I remember as my first purchase for the Windsor flat. I remember working at that table, when it was new and smooth as glass, the sash windows flung open to spring sunshine, the kitchen smelling of daffodils and chopped onions; and a few trial words going down on paper, words scented with furniture polish. I have a nervous sort of nostalgia for any surface I have written a book on, or even half a book; I think the words, for better or worse, have sunk into the grain of the wood. But the pine table is bashed and battered now, its surface gouged and its legs wobbling; I am touched by fellow feeling. I pat it for the last time: good table, good table. I don't watch it leave the house. It's going to a good home in my brother's workshop: light duties, an honourable retirement.

Owl Cottage sold within an hour of going on the market. One of Mr Ewing's ladies rang, her voice astonished, to say were we happy to accept the asking price? I have never had anything before or since, that another person wanted so much. And as we pack up, we are rushed, a little flustered; we hadn't thought we would have to quit so soon.

My mother arrives. Now we are going to do something difficult, which is to clear the loft. Some boxes were stowed up there by Jack when my parents first arrived in the county, and left there; now no one can remember what is in them.

When I went to Africa, I left a box of my own in the eaves of my parents' house. In it was my *Complete Works of Shakespeare*, which they had bought me (to keep me quiet) when I was ten. Even when it

was new it was cheap; but what did I care? It was
bound in fraying black cloth, its paper was yellowing
and woody, its blurred type looked as if it were
running from the page; I loved that book. My child's
fingerprints were on every leaf of it. I felt as if it
talked back to me, as if I had exchanged breath
with it; no other Complete Works would ever be
the same. By the time I was leaving England the
book was nearly fifteen years old, it was falling apart,
its glue drying, its pages brittle; I still liked it too
much to trust it to sea freight. I knew that to pack
it in my suitcase – a book like a house brick, against
my allowance of twenty kilos – would be a little
ridiculous. Besides, I feared the effects on it of a
change of climate. 'I'll just store it in the eaves,'
I said, for the eaves were spacious, dry and cool.
In the box, also, was a bibliography for my French
Revolution book, kept in a humble school exercise
book with a stiff burgundy cover. I thought – and I
was right – that it wouldn't be much use to me where
I was going.

Three years later – around the time I went to St
George's to have my insides remodelled – I came
back to my parents' house to reclaim the box. The
Revolution book was with a publisher, and if it was
accepted I would need my bibliography, to help me
with editing and checking. I felt a sober, righteous
pleasure as I waited for it to emerge from the eaves,

and I anticipated opening my Shakespeare, wondering which passage I would alight on first. But the searchers drew a blank. They frowned, puzzled, and rubbed out of their hair the fine dust of accreted pigeon droppings. It must be in there somewhere, they said. They dived in again, bent double, and emerged rubbing their backs, shaking their heads. No box, no Shakespeare, nothing at all conforming to the description of a burgundy notebook with five years of my reading life in it. 'Oh, look again,' I begged. They did; they drew a blank. The family said, that's strange. Where oh where can Ilary's box be? Some suggested supernatural reasons for its disappearance. But I had my own theory. Shakespeare is bunk. History is bunk. Why are women always smiling? Smile, smile, smile.

So much for my box. Now, at Owl Cottage, Jack's boxes come down from the loft, the men's feet bouncing on the steel ladder. The boxes are heavy, covered in what looks like iron filings. We take them into the kitchen and wipe them down. One box contains a tidy stack of *National Geographic* magazines. We know the contents before we open it, because it is precisely labelled in Jack's fading hand. Another box seems to be full of old engineering textbooks. Why keep them, I wonder? But it's not for me to judge the quality of someone else's nostalgia. It is five years since his death. Soon after the funeral my mother packed up his watercolour paints, ready for me to use, at some unlikely date when I have the leisure. We framed what we could from his last sketchbook, anything that was nearly complete: sea, sand, clouds. We put the sketchbook away with the paints, and with it the pictures he must have been working on: another seascape, and what may be, emerging from the paper's weave, an apple tree under a darkening sky.

'Get another cloth,' I say. 'There's a whole big box of them, under the sink.' The textbooks – sad waste paper – we pile in a stack. Then out comes an edition of Creasey's *Decisive Battles*, which I gave Jack because of its fine binding and marbled endpapers – and which, surprisingly, he decided to read. Now comes – I laugh as it emerges – an ancient, grimy relic called *'An Analysis of English History: with Appendix and Maps.'* I pick it out of the box; as I try to open it, its pages fall like loose cards into my hand. Inside the cover is written 'Beryl A. White, 58 Bankbottom, Hadfield, Near Manchester, England'. Beryl, my heroine, my cousin after whom I named my pointy-headed doll! I shuffle the pages, I look at a few. Their content is only slightly familiar; but is this not the tale of my native land? The story begins in the days when all the main players are called Ethel, those days when the successor of Ethelfrith marries Ethelburga, daughter of Ethelbert: hilarious consequences ensue. I shuffle the pages again: 'War with France: this war arose from an unseemly jest.' Shuffle again: 'The skeletons of two children were found buried at the foot of a staircase ... Marlborough took the field, but owing to the extreme dilatoriness of the Dutch ...' The book – if it can be called a book, in its loose-leaf state – is full of moral judgements, against unseemly jesting and turning up late for the fight. King John died of a fever brought on by anxiety, which one sees was weak of him; the character of Mary Tudor, naturally mild, took a turn for the worse 'when she gave her hand to the Spaniard'.

I put down the Analysis regretfully, vowing I will get back to it. Here is another book of Beryl's, her name in pencil in a round baby hand. 'She must have it back,' my mother says. 'I'll keep it for her.' It is 'Alice' – both adventures – in a jacket of porridge-coloured canvas. Next – but why? – comes a copy of *Lorna Doone*, abridged for the young. It is the remnant of a set of miscellaneous nineteenth-century novels I had for Christmas, perhaps the year I was ten. The colophon is a silhouette of a man in a tall hat, holding by the hand a silhouette child; the publisher's name is Dean & Son. How has this one survived, when *Treasure Island* has gone, the only one of the set to have a yellow jacket; where is *Jane Eyre*, bound in dull green? I remember the first time I read *Jane Eyre*: probably every woman writer does, because you recognise, when you have hardly begun it, that you are reading a story about yourself. The books with their coloured bindings were passed on, down the family; I remember how my youngest brother liked *Children of the New Forest*. It had a peach-coloured binding; I thought it was tedious, myself. *Kidnapped* came in dark-blue. I knew by heart its opening lines and, running through my memory, the words still affect me with a shiver of trepidation: 'I will begin the story of my adventures with a certain morning early in the month of June, the year of grace 1751, when I took the key for the last time out of the door of my father's house.' Like a wimp, like a girl, I wanted David Balfour to stay at home, with the kindly minister Mr Campbell, with his dead parents who lay in the churchyard under the rowan trees. The plot would never have got beyond its second page, if it had stood to me: its hero would never have left Essendean. I loved and trusted Alan Breck, his bantam swagger, his defiance of logic and the odds; but I worried about David and his welfare, much more than I worried about Jane Eyre, who, in my opinion, had stitched Rochester's eyes shut long before he went blind.

It is summer at Owl Cottage; light bounces on the black-and-white tiles of the kitchen floor. I put my arms, briefly, around the shoulders of my mother and my brother's wife. The box we are dipping into seems deeper than we thought, darker and fustier. Almost at the bottom of it, we find one of Jack's own books – one of those that came with him when he moved into our house at Brosscroft. It is *Out with Romany*, its title almost illegible now, its cover, which I remember as green, now faded to grey. It is illustrated with naïve woodcuts: a hedgehog, a bird's nest, hares dancing. We pass it from hand to hand. I'd like it, says my brother's wife, I like these pictures. Yes, take it, love, my mother says. Then last of all comes the vast tome of Tennyson, square and brown like a well-packed parcel, like a parcel that has been left in a sorting office for thirty years. I open it, and the odour of decay rises up, so powerful and bitter that it seems like the smell of burning. For a moment I stand, shaken, recalling this book in my child's hands: it was old then, the pages freckled with butter-coloured marks. 'Can I have this?' I ask. 'It must be middle age, you know, but I've been wanting to reread Tennyson lately.' I open the book, and my fingertips turn grey as I leaf through it.

> When cats run home and light is come,
> And dew is cold upon the ground ...

My mother, standing next to me, brushes my elbow; silently, heads bent over the empty box, we begin to cry.

October 2000: moving day at last. The sales of our two houses have been tied up neatly, completion of both on the same morning. Owl Cottage has been packed up by removal men; I couldn't stand to do it myself, to turn the key for the last time and leave Jack's baffled spirit locked in the shell of the house. At our Disneyland villa, as our furniture vanishes into the removal van, our neighbours, their children and their friends spread out over the garden, brooms and vacuum cleaners held like bayonets across their chests, ready for the charge. They have taken down a fence panel between the two gardens to give themselves access; as soon as the phone rings, as soon as the word from the lawyers comes through, they storm down the slope of the lawn and pour through the french windows, mob-handed. I have to plead for a safe corner in the house, for a twenty-minute respite, till the cats and I can be collected, for we are going last. I sit on the bathroom floor, the door locked against the mob, waiting, the minutes ebbing away, talking to the cats to soothe them, while they fume and moan in their travelling cages and rattle the bars. By the time I come downstairs, and walk out of the front door for the last time, the neighbours have got their furniture in place, their milk in the fridge, their food in the cupboards. It is theirs already, and they fit it; I cannot believe this house ever belonged to me. It has four children in it; solid, squalling, overexcited, ready for a showdown about who gets which room. The cats shake their fists at them, and curse as I hand over the spare door keys:

as the tailgate of the car slams on their bawling, the house becomes history.

The place we live in now is an apartment in a converted lunatic asylum. It was built in the 1860s, one of a loop of great institutions flung around London to catch and contain its burgeoning mad population, the melancholic and the syphilitic, the damaged and the deluded, the people who had forgotten their manners and the people who had forgotten their names.

Aren't you afraid of ghosts? visitors say. But I smile and shake my head; I say, not I. Not I: not here: not now.

We are on the top floor; but a spiral staircase leads even higher, to a small square room in the clock tower. We are the keepers of the gargoyles that guard the roofs, and we have a long view over the country, over the city of Guildford, dropped into the landscape like an egg into a dish: to a distant, fuzzy line of uplands that, on rainy days, when cloud thickens and almost obscures it, I can easily imagine is the moorland of my childhood.

Two wings of the old building have been preserved and converted, but thousands of houses have been built on the asylum's land. It is hard to believe that seven years ago it was open fields. An elderly man who grew up in the district told me what this countryside was like, before the mechanical diggers moved in. It was an area of market gardens and plant nurseries, and open land cut up with streams and ditches, into which, when he was a boy and out rabbiting, he would invariably fall; and pick his way home, at twilight, half drowned and dripping, to be shouted at by his mother. He was a good talker, and I found myself sliding, in imagination, into the country that he had shown me, so that it became a part of my own terrain.

Now on light clear nights, I sometimes go out on to the balcony; the clock face hangs above me like a second moon, lighting up the flickering tongues of the gargoyles, stone saureans leaning out into darkness and space. It is quiet up here: except for the background purr of travelling cars, on the circular road that holds the new houses, the new families, in a loose, careless embrace. I wrap myself in a blanket, and rest my forehead on the balcony's freezing rail, and think about what I have lost and what I have gained. For me, the balcony is the best thing about the asylum. I am out there in all weathers, looking over the army land that is the last remnant of the unpopulated place this used to be. Sometimes, at dawn or at dusk, I pick out from the gloom – I think I do – a certain figure, traversing those rutted fields in a hushed and pearly light, picking a way among the treacherous rivulets and the concealed ditches. It is a figure shrouded in a cloak, bearing certain bulky objects wrapped in oilcloth, irregular in shape: not heavy but awkward to carry. This figure is me; these shapes, hidden in their wrappings, are books that, God willing, I am going to write. But when was God ever willing? And what is this dim country, what is this tenuous path I lose so often – where am I trying to get to, when the light is so uncertain? Steps to Literature, I think; I have tottered one or two. I move back from the window, dawn or dusk; I think of other houses, which seem not so long ago.

At 20 Brosscroft, the windows printed on our curtains are alight from within, their flowerpots spilling scarlet blooms, the candle flames swelling, flickering boldly against the fading northern afternoon. The table is laid, and the dead are peering at their place cards, and shuffling into their chairs, and shaking out their napkins, waiting, expectant, for whatever is next. Food or entertainment, it's all one to the eyeless, the shrivelled and the thin: to the ones who have crossed into the land where only the living can provide their light. I will always look after you, I want to say, however long you have been gone. I will always feed you, and try to keep you entertained; and you must do the same for me. This is your daughter Ilary speaking, and this is her book.